PART V. REVIEW AND BANKING

PART VI. APPENDICES

PART I

The Use of Objective Questions

1

What is an Objective Test?

Definition

An objective test is one in which all the questions are so devised that they can be marked without any subjective judgment on the part of the marker. Students do not compose their own answers but select the correct answer or answers from a given list (as in Example 1.1); the correct answer is predetermined, so that all markers mark to exactly the same rules and each student receives exactly the same score no matter who marks his script.

It should be noted that it is *only* the marking of the test which is objective. The content and balance of the test remain matters for the judgment of the subject experts.

'Objective tests' should not be confused with behavioural or examination 'objectives' (sometimes divided into 'general' and 'specific' objectives), which are a means of stating the syllabus content in terms of what the student should be able to do by the end of the course.

Types of Objective Question

There are a number of types of objective question (or 'item' as they are often termed).

EXAMPLE

1.1 *Mechanical Engineering Maintenance*

In certain circumstances plain bearings are preferred to roller- or ball-bearings because they:
(a)   can be used at higher speeds
(b)   produce less friction
(c)   will take greater loads at lower speeds
(d)   produce more friction.

3

The most widely used is *multiple-choice*, as shown in Example 1.1. The question (which may be in the form of a question, with a question mark, or of an incomplete statement) is followed by four (or sometimes five) possible answers, of which only *one* is correct. The student has to select the correct answer.

In a *multiple-response* question, as shown in Example 1.2, the number of possible answers (or 'options') is larger and *more than one* is correct; the student has to indicate which are correct. In many cases the beginning of the question (or 'stem') states how many answers are required; Example 1.2 would then begin 'Which THREE of the following verbs . . .'

Example 1.3 is a *matching* question. Students have to match the items in List 2 with those in List 1, using the 'match panel' provided.

In an *assertion/reason* question, such as Example 1.4, the student has to decide on the truth of each of the two statements and whether there is a connection between them.

EXAMPLES

1.2   *Further Education Teachers*

Which of the following verbs would be acceptable for use in a list of specific objectives?

(a)   understand
(b)   state
(c)   draw
(d)   solder
(e)   know
(f)   appreciate.

1.3   *Carpentry and Joinery*

Match the tools in List 2 with the operations for which they would be used in List 1.

List 1	List 2
(A) straight cutting	(1) spindle
(B) circular cutting	(2) circular saw
(C) moulding	(3) mortiser
(D) end profiling	(4) tenoner
	(5) bandsaw

A	B	C	D

A *true/false* question, such as Example 1.5, asks the student simply to decide whether the statement given is true or false.

Short-answer questions, such as Example 1.6, are sometimes classified as objective questions, but they are not really so. Even an apparently straight-forward question like this example can require some subjective judgment in the marking. The expected answer is the watt; markers would have to decide whether to accept 'wat' or even 'what' as an acceptable answer, and what to do about an answer of 'kilowatt'. Most short-answer questions require much more judgment in marking than this.

The relative merits of the different types of truly objective questions are discussed in Chapter 4 and techniques for writing types other than multiple-choice are considered in Chapter 8. Most of the discussion in this book will, however, centre on multiple-choice questions which are the most versatile type as well as the most widely used.

==

EXAMPLES

1.4 *Photography*

ASSERTION   REASON
The dilution of sulphuric acid   BECAUSE   when sulphuric acid is mixed
should only be carried out by   with water there is a strong
adding the acid slowly to the   exothermic reaction.
water

With reference to the above, which of the following is correct?
(a)   Both assertion and reason are true statements and the reason is a correct explanation of the assertion.
(b)   Both assertion and reason are true statements, but the reason is not a correct explanation of the assertion.
(c)   The assertion is true but the reason is a false statement.
(d)   The assertion is false, but the reason is a true statement.
(e)   Both assertion and reason are false statements.

1.5 *Agriculture*

Matted turf in a pasture is normally the result of soil acidity.

TRUE/FALSE

1.6 *Electrical Craft*

What is the unit of electrical power?

Abilities Tested by Objective Questions

Like other written tests, objective tests can assess the student's knowledge and his use of this knowledge ('cognitive abilities'), but not his practical skill ('psychomotor abilities'). It is convenient to divide cognitive abilities into a number of levels; the best-known scheme for doing this is that devised by B. S. Bloom, who identified six levels of ability of which the lowest three, factual recall, comprehension and application, are readily assessed by means of objective questions.

Recall of Facts questions, such as Example 1.7, assess simply the student's ability to remember what he has been taught.

Comprehension questions assess his understanding of this information, the reasons why something is done (as in Example 1.8), the translation of information from one form of presentation to another (e.g. from graphical to verbal) and so on.

In an *application* question, the student is required to go further and to use his knowledge and understanding to solve a problem which is new to him. In Example 1.9 the student is asked to use his understanding of components and circuits to say what will happen in the given circuit if the capacitor fails.

Many further education courses require only a small measure, if any, of the three higher abilities identified by Bloom, i.e. analysis, synthesis and evaluation. Synthesis is the most commonly required of the three and concerns the student's skill in combining knowledge from different subject

---

EXAMPLES

1.7   *Business Studies*

Which of the following is in the public sector?
(a)   Joint Stock Board
(b)   Engineering Employers' Federation
(c)   Building Society
(d)   Regional Gas Board.

1.8   *Food and Family*

Blanching is necessary when freezing most vegetables to:
(a)   kill all harmful bacteria
(b)   inactivate enzymes
(c)   preserve vitamin C
(d)   improve the flavour.

areas to create a novel product or communication; for example the design of a component to a given specification. This ability is not readily assessed by means of objective questions, as there is no single correct solution to any problem set.

The Technician Education Council identifies four abilities within the cognitive domain, information (corresponding to factual recall), comprehension, application and invention (which corresponds approximately to synthesis).

End-of-course Examinations and In-course Tests

Objective questions may be used both in end-of-course examinations and in tests held at intervals during the course. An examination held at the end of the course or unit is usually of longer duration (at least one hour) and covers the whole of the syllabus for the course or unit; each of a series of in-course (or phase) tests would be shorter (about half an hour) and cover only that part of

---

EXAMPLE

1.9   *Electrical and Electronic Craft*

In the circuit shown, the main effect of capacitor C1 going open circuit will be:
(a)   a reduction of the output signal voltage
(b)   an increase of the output signal voltage
(c)   an increase in the d.c. current
(d)   a decrease in the d.c. current.

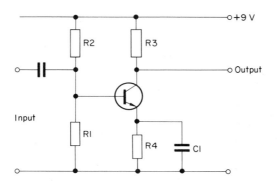

the syllabus which had just been taught. However, the principles of planning the test and producing the questions are the same for both end-of-course examinations and in-course tests.

2

Why Choose Objective Tests?

A good assessment method is:

valid,   i.e. it measures appropriate knowledge and abilities;

reliable,   i.e. it applies a consistent standard of measurement to all students and in all years;

efficient,   i.e. it makes best use of resources and of lecturer and student time;

beneficial rather than harmful in its *side-effects* upon the course of study leading up to it.

Well-designed objective tests, appropriately used, can contribute to all four aspects of a good assessment, and this explains why they have greatly increased in popularity in recent years.

The main advantages of objective tests are listed below. Of these, Nos. 1 to 6 relate mainly to the validity of the assessment, Nos. 7 to 9 to its reliability, Nos. 10 to 12 to its efficiency and Nos. 13 and 14 to its side-effects. It should be noted, however, that objective tests do not have a monopoly of the virtues and that some advantages of objective tests can be shared, at least in part, by other methods of assessment. Short-answer and structured questions, for example, can give consistent syllabus coverage from year to year.

1. Good Syllabus Coverage

Because objective questions can be answered more quickly than equivalent constructed-answer questions, more questions can be asked in a given period of time. Consequently, objective questions can cover the syllabus better than conventional questions.

2. Appropriate Balance of Abilities Tested

An objective test may be designed to have an appropriate proportion of
questions testing recall of facts, comprehension and application as well as
understanding of drawings and graphs where these are required. Example 2.1
shows a question testing understanding of a drawing and Example 2.2 shows
how comprehension of graphs may be tested in an objective question.

===

EXAMPLE

2.1   *Welding Craft*

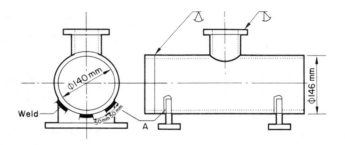

The diagram above shows a component fabricated from stabilised austenitic stainless steel
sheet 3 mm thick. The fillet welds on the support brackets should have 5 mm leg length
with 50 mm intermittent welds as shown. The symbol at 'A' to communicate this information should be:

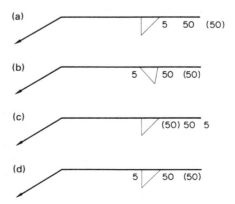

For assessing recall and comprehension of specific information, objective, short-answer and structured questions are more suitable than other forms of assessment; project-type exercises and course-work assessment which allow the use of reference material make it impossible to test whether the student actually remembers a particular fact.

3. Consistent Syllabus Coverage from Year to Year

An objective test is set in accordance with a specification (see Example 2.3) which determines the number of questions to be set on each syllabus topic and ability. This ensures that the syllabus coverage remains the same from year to year and assists reliability as well as validity.

EXAMPLE

2.2 *Motor Vehicle Craft*

The graph below shows the steady-speed fuel consumption of a car in fourth gear and in overdrive. Which of the following conditions gives the best economy?

(a)   fourth gear at 40 mile/h

(b)   fourth gear at 60 mile/h

(c)   overdrive at 60 mile/h

(d)   overdrive at 70 mile/h

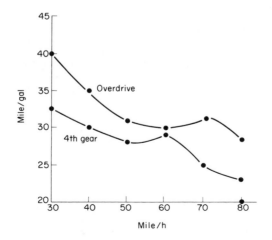

4. Compulsory Questions

Because all questions in an objective test are compulsory, all students answer questions on the same syllabus topics and abilities. In a traditional six-out-of-ten paper, two students may attempt questions on almost completely different topics.

5. Results Less Influenced by Irrelevant Abilities

In an essay examination, a student's result is considerably affected by his skills of self-expression, of selection of relevant facts and of organising his material into an essay. These skills are not required in an objective test, so that the student's score reflects his technical knowledge and understanding much more closely. Nor does an objective test require skill in sketching, drawing or the production of graphs. These skills are sometimes required in a traditional examination, not because they are intended as ends in themselves, but as a medium for the expression of the student's technical knowledge. The examination may then be measuring and awarding marks for abilities which the syllabus writers did not intend.

EXAMPLE

2.3 *Specification for an Objective Test in Welding Craft*

Topic	Number of questions to be set testing			
	Recall	Comprehension	Application	Total
1 Safety	2	2	0	4
2 Principles of welding and cutting	4	7	5	16
3 Equipment and consumables	3	6	4	13
4 Standards of welding	1	2	2	5
5 Oxy-gas welding	0	0	0	0
6 Manual metal-arc and gas-shielded welding	1	3	5	9
7 Faults and fault correction	1	5	0	6
8 Communication	2	3	2	7
Totals	14	28	18	60

The objective test's independence of such skills as drawing, writing English and selection of relevant information is, of course, only an advantage if they are indeed irrelevant to the abilities being assessed. If such skills form part of the course of instruction, then objective questions cannot constitute the *only* means of assessment. They may, however, still have a place in conjunction with other methods.

An objective test places less emphasis on speed of working than do many traditional examinations. Although a paper containing 60, 80 or even 100 questions may appear daunting, there is usually ample time for the student to work through the paper and give a considered answer to each question. Because he or she does not have to write out the answer, a larger proportion of the examination time can be spent in thinking.

6. Precise Questions

Competently written objective questions can be very precise, so testing specific aspects of the student's knowledge and understanding. Example 2.4 is a precise question. Example 2.5 shows how an examiner might attempt to test the same topic in a short-answer question; a wide range of answers would probably be received and many might fail to include the information which the examiner was really seeking. Example 2.6 is even less precise and would place considerable emphasis on the student's essay-writing skills.

EXAMPLE

2.4 *Food and Family*

Which ONE of the following foods freezes successfully?
(a) broad beans
(b) cucumber
(c) garlic sausage
(d) boiled eggs.

2.5 *Food and Family*

What types of food can be frozen successfully?

2.6 *Food and Family*

Discuss the contribution which the use of a home freezer can make to the variety and economy of a family's diet.

7. Reliable Marking

By far the most important advantage of objective questions is their objectivity, i.e. the reliability with which they are marked. Apart from occasional errors, two markers will always award the same mark to a student's answers to an objective paper, which is by no means always true of a constructed-answer paper. Example 2.5, which is admittedly a rather poor short-answer question, would elicit a variety of different answers ranging from 'meat and vegetables' to 'broad beans, runner beans, peas, brussel sprouts', etc. Markers would find it difficult to evaluate the relative merits of the answers given, and even with the aid of a marking scheme, two markers would be unlikely to give the same marks to the same scripts. Example 2.6 would give an even greater variety of both content and structure of answers, and would be correspondingly more difficult to mark consistently. Example 2.4, on the other hand, could be marked reliably by anyone supplied with an answer key.

Reliability of marking may appear to be less of a problem in a single-college examination where only one marker is involved, but it is of real importance if the questions are to be banked and reused; comparison of the performance of students in two years is only relevant if the marking standard has remained the same.

8. Consistent Standard from Year to Year

If the questions are analysed and satisfactory ones banked for reuse, as they should be, the standard of the paper can be kept consistent from year to year. Reusing questions of known difficulty makes it possible to compare students' results accurately from year to year—something which cannot be done with certainty if it is necessary to rely on the subjective impressions of one or two markers. As the marking is objective it follows that any unexpected performance on the paper is due to the students, not to the difficulty of the paper or the severity of the marking.

9. Assessment of the Student's Own Work

With course-work or a project it may sometimes be difficult to ensure that the work submitted is the student's own. Sometimes, of course, it may be a desirable part of the task for the student to collect information from outside sources, written and otherwise. If, however, it is necessary to test what information the student himself has remembered and understood and can apply, an examination or test offers a better means of doing so than a course-work assessment.

10. Efficient Use of Student Examination Time

Because objective questions can be answered relatively quickly, without the student needing to write out his answer, more questions can be asked in the time available and a higher proportion of the syllabus covered. Indeed, an objective test may be of shorter duration than a constructed-answer test covering the same ground. Student examination time is therefore used more efficiently.

11. Efficient Marking

Marking can be done quite quickly, using a template or some form of machine, thus freeing the lecturer for other tasks. Since the marking key is fixed there is no need for any measures to coordinate the marking of a number of markers. However, the ease of marking is partly offset by the greater difficulty in setting objective questions, so that their use may be restricted to situations where the number of examinees is relatively large. On grounds of efficiency alone, objective questions would probably not be chosen for examinations with less than 100—200 students per year. Below that level they may be chosen for other reasons, but only if the resources available are sufficient to ensure that questions of good quality are set—this is a point which will be considered in more detail later (see Chapter 3).

12. Question Banking

A system of analysing and banking good questions for reuse ensures that the effort put into writing the questions is not wasted; this is important in view of the extra effort which goes into writing a good objective question. The bank needs periodic revision and additions to ensure that questions which become out of date are excluded and that there is not a frequent repetition of a few questions. However, there is still an overall saving of setting time as a result of banking.

13. Discouragement of 'Question Spotting'

Since there is good syllabus coverage in each examination set, there is no point in 'question spotting' to try to guess which topics will appear in the next paper. Consequently students and lecturers are encouraged to cover the whole syllabus.

14. Rapid Feedback

Because the marking is much easier than for a traditional paper, results can be issued more quickly. Students who have taken in-course objective tests can be told which areas they need to revise further and there may be enough time for them to do so and take another test before moving on to study the next topic.

APPLICATION

1. Review the advantages of objective examinations or tests with which you are concerned. Are there any advantages of objective testing which are not being realised in these examinations?

2. List the non-objective examinations or tests with which you are concerned.

   (a) What advantages would be gained by changing to the use of objective questions?

   (b) What disadvantages, if any, would there be?

3

Can Objective Tests be Improved?

The reader will not be surprised to learn that the short answer to this question is 'Yes'. There can be very few objective tests indeed which are perfect; many are poor or contain a proportion of poor questions. These give objective questions a bad name and, in the minds of some critics, outweigh the undoubted advantages which this type of testing can offer. Good objective questions are rather more difficult to write than good constructed-answer ones and poor questions are much more obviously poor—partly because the possible answers are available for scrutiny as well as the questions.

Since objective questions have a high degree of reliability, most of the possible improvements suggested below relate to validity. However, inclusion of poor questions or failure to follow recommended procedures can lead to a reduction in the reliability of an objective test.

The following suggestions can help to improve the quality of objective tests.

Do not Attempt to Use Objective Tests for Unsuitable Knowledge or Abilities

Objective questions are not capable of testing the student's ability to draw, sketch, produce graphs, write essays or follow through long calculations and there should be no attempt to use them in this way. Objective questions can, of course, test understanding of drawings, graphs and English and ability to perform short calculations; they are indeed a very good way of doing so. However, it is essential to be sure at the beginning that this is in fact the aspect which *ought* to be tested. In some circumstances it may be appropriate to have two assessment components:

(a) an objective paper to test understanding over a wide area of the syllabus;

(b) a constructed-answer paper, project or course-work assessment to test the ability to perform the required task, e.g. draw, sketch, write essays.

Objective questions, carefully set, can test application of facts as well as their recall and understanding. They are not, however, a good way of testing synthesis—the ability to assemble and relate a range of information to produce a new work, which could, for example, be a design, an essay or a computer program. Some testing specialists maintain that objective questions *can* be used in this way, but the number of people who claim to be able to set satisfactory objective questions to test synthesis is very small and does not include this author.

Do not Attempt to Begin Objective Testing with Insufficient Resources

The resources needed to produce valid and reliable objective questions are mainly human. Even an experienced writer of items (objective questions) finds it difficult to produce enough good questions for a 60- or 80-item test within a reasonable period of time. An inexperienced writer may have difficulty producing ten good questions. Including substandard questions to make up the required number, because time is short, only detracts from the value of the test or examination. It follows that, unless circumstances are exceptional, a lecturer should not embark on a programme of objective testing single-handed, and a pair of lecturers should only do so if they are experienced in the techniques and the examinations are not required more than twice a year. In most situations a minimum of three active and reasonably experienced writers is desirable. The writers must, of course, be familiar with the course and the level of students and fully conversant with the subject matter.

Item Writers must be Trained

Writing objective items is an art which requires a knowledge of the principles, much practice and feedback from others. Although a book such as this provides a useful basis, it should be supplemented by practice in actually writing items, which should then be submitted to a second person for comment. In this way the writer can be shown shortcomings in the items and helped to improve them.

Chapter 7 of this book outlines some basic principles of item writing and Chapter 9 considers some more sophisticated techniques.

Questions should be Vetted

Whether the writer is a novice or an 'old hand', any questions written for an examination, a test or even a pretest, should be 'edited' by at least one other person familiar with the subject matter, the course and the techniques of writing items. Many items which seem clear and uncontroversial to the writer prove to have unsuspected pitfalls, and editing can help to overcome these problems before the questions are presented to students for answering.

Even if the individual questions have already been edited and perhaps pretested, the final version of the paper should also be subjected to a second opinion. This editing of the complete paper should seek to ensure that there is an appropriate balance of questions and that questions do not overlap or answer one another.

Chapter 10 suggests procedures for editing and lists points to be considered when editing the paper as a whole and individual questions within it.

The Paper should be Appropriately Balanced

In any one paper or test there should be an appropriate balance of questions on different syllabus topics and of questions testing the different abilities of recall, comprehension and application. This is, of course, ensured if an appropriate specification is prepared and followed. Although it may sometimes be difficult to distinguish with certainty between questions testing different abilities, it is important to make the attempt. Questions testing recall tend to be much easier to write than others and there is a temptation to ignore comprehension and application; the end product is likely to be a paper which is trite.

Do not Ask Trivial, Irrelevant or Obvious Questions

This is an obvious point which is often ignored—particularly if the writers or compilers are having difficulty finding the right number of questions. Faults in questions are covered in more detail in Chapter 7, but it is worth mentioning here some of the more serious:

(a) questions testing knowledge which is trivial or (as in Example 3.1) irrelevant to the course;

(b) questions which test only knowledge of jargon or which (as Example 3.2) can readily be guessed by the student with good understanding of English rather than of the course's subject matter;

(c) questions which test mental agility, rather than technical knowledge (Example 3.3 with its double negatives comes into this category);

(d) silly distractors, like (c) and, to a lesser extent, (d) in Example 3.4;

(e) questions, as in Example 3.5, which are just too easy. (However, it is important that safety questions should be asked, so an improved version of such a question might well be used.);

(f) multiple-choice questions which have more than one possible answer; in Example 3.6 any answer could be argued to be correct, depending upon the circumstances.

Make Use of Statistical Analysis

As described in Chapters 14 and 15, statistical analysis can provide a most useful indication of how the paper or test as a whole has been answered and how individual questions within it have performed. Statistical analysis should

---

EXAMPLES

3.1 *Further Education Teachers*

Which of the following is the basic unit of heredity?

(a) the gene

(b) the chromosome

(c) RNA

(d) DNA.

3.2 *Horticulture*

Undesirably constricted root systems in nursery stock grown in containers are often due to insufficient:

(a) carbohydrate production

(b) nutrients in the compost

(c) water in the compost

(d) space in the container.

be regarded as a tool, furnishing evidence on which decisions can be made, and not as a master to be followed slavishly; however, it is foolish to go to the other extreme and to ignore the evidence of the statistics because it conflicts with the writer's preconceived ideas. Very low or negative discrimination figures, for example, are almost always an indication that something is amiss and should not be discounted lightly.

EXAMPLES

3.3 *Child Development*

Which of the following statements concerning child development are not true?
(1) A child under five is not usually ready for formal lessons.
(2) Five-year-olds have some difficulty distinguishing fact from fiction.
(3) Small children do not learn through play.
(4) Learning to read is the first priority for a child entering school.
(5) Reinforcement of good behaviour produces beneficial results.

    (a) 1 and 2 only
    (b) 3 and 4 only
    (c) 1, 4 and 5 only
    (d) 2, 3 and 4 only.

3.4 *Forestry*

An advantage of using small transplants in commercial forestry is that they:
(a) look attractive
(b) establish easily
(c) are more expensive
(d) are liable to browsing.

3.5 *Safety and First Aid*

The first action to take when a person is receiving an electric shock and is still connected to the supply is to:
(a) call an ambulance
(b) offer a hot sweet drink
(c) start artificial respiration
(d) disconnect the supply.

3.6 *Further Education Teachers*

One function of a tutor in a small group discussion is to:
(a) ensure a contribution from everyone
(b) give a clear and stimulating introduction
(c) clarify and expand points as they emerge
(d) make certain that the group arrive at some definite conclusions.

Do not Allow the Use of Objective Testing to Affect the Course Adversely

Objective questions are the most reliable assessment method and should not be used unless they are acceptably valid for the course in question. However, there are some courses for which objective questions are a suitable assessment method but do not cover all the course aims; for example the course might also aim to encourage right attitudes or to improve students' skills in self-expression. Normally, such aims should be assessed by an additional examination component (a constructed-answer paper or a course-work assessment), but occasionally this may be inappropriate; attitudes are notoriously difficult to assess, and it may be considered undesirable to make the student's result for the course dependent upon his communication skills. In such instances the lecturers should beware of the temptation to drop these objectives from the course simply because they are not covered in the assessment.

The remaining chapters of this book give advice on various aspects of preparing and using objective questions. Following this advice, but adapting where necessary to suit the needs of the individual course or subject, should result in tests and examinations which are both valid and reliable.

APPLICATION
Review the arrangements for an objective test with which you are concerned.

1. Is the test assessing the right abilities? Are any desirable abilities (e.g. drawing, calculations) being omitted from the assessment of the course because only objective testing is used?

2. Are any desirable abilities being omitted from the teaching of the course because they are not assessed?

3. Are there enough competent question writers?

4. Have the writers had adequate training and experience?

5. Are the questions thoroughly edited before pretesting or use?

6. Is there a specification determining coverage of both topics and abilities? Is it followed?

7. Are all the questions included in the test of good quality?

8. Is statistical analysis obtained and used to eliminate poor questions and to maintain a consistent standard of award?

PART II

Planning the Test

4

Which Type of Objective Question?

An important early stage in planning an objective examination or test is to decide what type or types of objective question are to be used. It will almost certainly be found necessary to use multiple-choice questions. Should any of the other types (multiple-response, assertion/reason, matching, true/false) be used as well? Item writers' opinions on this tend to range from 'multiple-choice can do it all perfectly well' to 'a variety of types should be used to test different abilities'. Since the characteristics of the various types differ somewhat, we shall look at them in greater detail.

Multiple-choice

A multiple-choice question, as shown in Example 4.1, consists of a stem, which poses the problem, one correct answer (the 'key') and three or four incorrect answers (the 'distractors'); the key and distractors are together termed the 'options'. The stem may be a question ending in a question mark, as in Example 4.1, or an incomplete statement, as in Example 4.2.

Multiple-choice questions are undoubtedly the most versatile type of objective question, capable of testing simple recall of facts, comprehension (as in Example 4.2) or application (as in Example 4.1), understanding of drawings, simple calculations, or understanding of graphs. As described in Chapter 9, more sophisticated versions of the multiple-choice question may be devised to cater for problems in item writing or to provide more searching questions.

A common criticism of multiple-choice questions, as of other types of objective question, is that the student with no knowledge may guess the answer; in a four-option multiple-choice question he has a 25% chance of being right. This is not such a serious problem as it might seem; the student with no knowledge at all should not be sitting the examination; if he does sit

EXAMPLES

4.1 *Instrument Production Craft*

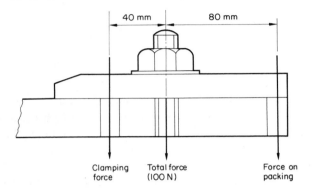

The clamping arrangement shown above has a clamping force ratio of 2:1. How far should the bolt be moved to increase the clamping ratio to 4:1?

(a)   4 mm

(b)   8 mm

(c)   12 mm

(d)   16 mm.

4.2 *Horticulture*

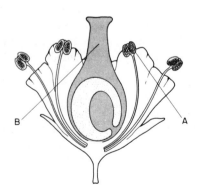

The function of the part labelled B in the above diagram is to:

(a)   produce nectar

(b)   attract insects

(c)   produce pollen

(d)   receive pollen.

it, his most likely score is 25%—well below the normal pass mark. The student who knows 60% of the answers usually deserves to pass anyway, whether or not he guesses on the remaining questions. The real problem is with the student who knows say 30 of 100 questions. If he guesses blindly on the remaining 70 his most likely score is 47 or 48 (30 + 70/4) and if he is lucky in his guesses he may score over 50 (which may be the pass mark). The desirability of applying a correction for guessing is discussed in Chapter 5. In general it is best to recognise that there will be an element of guessing and to make allowances for it when considering where to put the pass mark; however, guesses are less likely to be 'blind' than to be informed; the student eliminates one or two distractors which he knows to be wrong and then makes a choice between the remainder. Careful construction of the questions, particularly the distractors, can give questions which discriminate sharply in favour of those who know the answer and lead those who do not know to choose a distractor rather than to guess blindly. The test should not include questions which are both difficult and undiscriminating, as it is on such questions that students are most likely to guess—students do not guess on questions which they know or on those where they are confident that the answer is one of the distractors.

Not all multiple-choice questions have four options and the test constructor must decide in advance how many options there are to be. The number should be the same for all items in the test. Three options would be too few, as the possibility of obtaining the correct answer by blind guessing would then be 33.3%. The use of five options would reduce the chances of guessing correctly to 20% but have the disadvantage that such questions are more difficult to set. It is sometimes hard to find three good distractors; to find four for every item in the test would be almost impossible. Including a poor distractor to make up the number would destroy the object of the exercise; students would recognise it as implausible and discount it, thus effectively reducing the question to a four-option one. In practice the use of four options (key and three distractors) is a good compromise between ease of setting and reduced likelihood of guessing.

Multiple-response

A multiple-response question such as Example 4.3 resembles a multiple-choice one in having a stem and a series of options; they differ in that the multiple-response question has a larger number of options and has more than one key or correct answer. Students may be told to indicate the two, three or four correct answers, as in the example, or may be left to decide for themselves how many answers to select; the latter is more difficult. The usual method of marking multiple-response questions is to award a mark only if the student has answered everything correctly. This has the advantage that the likelihood of guessing correctly is greatly reduced—to 6.7% if the student is told to mark two or four answers out of six, to 5% if he is told to mark three out of six and to 1.75% if he is told to mark 'more than one' of six. It has the disadvantage that the student who is partly right gets no credit at all. If he has correctly marked two of three answers required, he still gets no mark. Awarding one mark for each correct answer would make the question much more like a multiple-choice one and increase the chances of obtaining a mark by guessing.

Multiple-response questions share some of the advantages of multiple-choice, but are less flexible. They are useful where there are several correct answers, all of which need to be known, and few plausible distractors. There are, however, many situations where this is not the case and where multiple-response questions are not practicable. Because the student needs two or three pieces of information in order to answer the whole question correctly, multiple-response questions tend in practice to be more difficult than multiple-choice.

Within any one examination or test, the number of options in the multiple-response questions should be kept consistent. Four or five options would be too few, making the questions too close to the multiple-choice type. More than eight options would make the questions too confusing for the students and too difficult to write. Six or eight options would be a suitable number. The number of correct answers out of the six or eight may vary. Students should, however, be told at the beginning of the paper that the number

---

EXAMPLE

4.3 *Cookery*

Which THREE of the following should be prepared as an accompaniment to roast leg of pork?

(a) apple slices
(b) apple sauce
(c) thyme and parsley stuffing
(d) sage and onion stuffing
(e) roast gravy
(f) thickened gravy.

correct will vary or be told in each question how many to select. The latter is usually better as it emphasises that it is not simply a multiple-choice question, with only one correct answer, and it assists the student. It is particularly important to state how many answers are expected if there are shades of rightness in the options rather than a clear division between right and wrong; in general, however, multiple-response questions are better avoided if the possible answers do not divide clearly into right and wrong.

Assertion/Reason

In an assertion/reason question, such as Example 4.4, the stem consists of an assertion and a reason and the options ask the student to judge the truth of each and whether there is a causal connection between them. The wording of the options may differ slightly from that shown in the example, but should be consistent for all questions of the type in any one test. Assertion/reason questions test mainly comprehension, but also require a degree of logic and semantic understanding which makes them unsuitable for students of lower ability. They can play a useful part in assessment, but are too limited to be the only type of objective question used in a test.

Questions of this type are not as easy to write as might be supposed. Each of the standard options must be plausible, so it follows that both the assertion and the reason must be statements which may be true or false in their own right and that there must be a potential, but not over-obvious, connection between them. Students attempting to answer the question may encounter problems if the reason given is one of several contributory factors which

---

EXAMPLE

4.4 *Welding Craft*

ASSERTION		REASON
Low carbon steel can be welded successfully by oxy-acetylene without the use of a flux	BECAUSE	the oxide has a higher melting point than the parent metal.

With reference to the above, which of the following is correct?

(a) Both assertion and reason are true statements and the reason is a correct explanation of the assertion.

(b) Both assertion and reason are true statements, but the reason is not a correct explanation of the assertion.

(c) The assertion is true but the reason is a false statement.

(d) The assertion is false but the reason is a true statement.

(e) Both assertion and reason are false statements.

account for the assertion; the students may be in doubt as to whether the reason is the most important factor (in which case the answer would be (a)) or a subsidiary factor (in which case the answer would be (b)).

Matching

A matching question, as in Example 4.5, consists of a stem, which gives instructions, and two lists, items in one list being matched to those in the other in accordance with the guidance given in the stem. The second list usually contains one extra item which is not used in the correct answer, so that the last of the pairings cannot be found by a process of elimination.

A mark is normally awarded only if all items are matched correctly. This means that the chances of obtaining a mark by guesswork alone are negligible (less than 1% if there are four items in one list and five in the other), but has two disadvantages.

(*a*) The students receives no credit if he knows some of the pairings but not all.

(*b*) There are so many possible combinations that the questions are virtually impossible to analyse in detail. There is therefore no information after the test on where, if at all, the students went wrong, and no basis on which to improve questions which give unexpected results.

Matching questions can be a useful way of testing recall of facts and of covering several pieces of information at once. They are much less versatile than multiple-choice questions and are less suitable for testing comprehension and application.

EXAMPLE

4.5 *Food and Family*

Match the food constituents in List 1 with the sources in List 2.

List 1   List 2
(A) iron   (1) fresh orange juice
(B) calcium   (2) cheese
(C) fibre   (3) fish
(D) iodine   (4) wholemeal flour
                                (5) egg yolk

A	B	C	D

Good matching questions are not always easy to write. Each of the items in List 2 should in theory be a plausible match for each of those in List 1, but this is difficult to achieve in practice. It is all too easy to include pairings which are obvious, so reducing the number of plausible combinations available to the student.

The number of items in the two lists need not necessarily be four and five but should be consistent within the test. Fewer items would make the questions too easy and 'guessable'. More than about six items in each list would make the question potentially confusing for the student and it would be difficult to find enough plausible items for each list. A good compromise is four and five or five and six in the two lists.

True/False

A true/false question, such as Example 4.6, consists of a single statement which the student must mark true or false. The use of this type of question is not recommended because there is a 50% chance of guessing the answer. Also it is difficult to write the statements so that they are undeniably correct (or incorrect) without including 'cue words' which give the answer away to the experienced test-taker. Words such as 'usually' and 'normally' often point to the statement being true (as in Example 4.7); words such as 'all', 'always' and 'never' often reveal a false statement (as in Example 4.8).

To give the same theoretical reliability, a test of true/false questions should contain twice as many items as a multiple-choice test—assuming that the items are all of good quality, without clues. Producing an adequate true/false

---

EXAMPLES

4.6 *Business Studies*

A credit customer must pay on delivery.

TRUE/FALSE

4.7 *Brickwork*

A compression joint should normally be placed below a bonder course.

TRUE/FALSE

4.8 *Electrical Installation*

All thermostats contain a permanent magnet.

TRUE/FALSE

test is therefore no easier, and in some ways harder, than producing a multiple-choice test. Some writers have tried to overcome the problem of guessing by using 'modified' true/false questions. In the type shown in Example 4.9 the student is asked to write in the correct words if he judges the statement to be false. In Example 4.10 he is asked to select an alternative. These devices cannot be considered very successful. Example 4.9 becomes a short-answer question requiring judgment in its marking and therefore not objective. Example 4.10 could just as well be asked in multiple-choice form.

Short Answer

Short-answer questions are not objective and should not be included within an objective paper.

Which Type or Types of Question?

Example 4.11 summarises the characteristics of the main types of objective question. The final decision on the type or types of question to use depends upon the nature of the subject matter and abilities to be assessed, and is a matter for the subject expert, but the following points should be borne in mind.

(a) It is most unlikely to be possible to cover the whole of the necessary subject matter and abilities without using some multiple-choice questions, since these are the most flexible type. The choice is therefore

---

EXAMPLES

4.9   *Furniture Craft*

Mark the following statement TRUE or FALSE. If you mark it FALSE, write in the space provided the words which should replace the underlined words.

The rails used in deep-stuffed chair frames are mainly jointed by <u>scarfed joints</u>.

TRUE/FALSE ....

4.10   *Furniture Craft*

Mark the following statement TRUE or FALSE. If you mark it FALSE, indicate which of the options provided below should replace the underlined words.

The rails used in deep-stuffed chair frames are mainly jointed by <u>scarfed joints</u>.

TRUE/FALSE

(a)   dowelled joints
(b)   dovetailed joints
(c)   halving joints.

between using multiple-choice alone and using a mixture of multiple-choice and other types of question.

(b) Assertion/reason are not usually suitable for students of lower ability (operative, craft and equivalent) and multiple-response and matching should be used with caution for such students, as they may be found confusing when used in the same paper as multiple-choice.

(c) The use of true/false questions is not recommended at all.

EXAMPLE

4.11 *Characteristics of Types of Objective Question*

	Guessing factor (%)	Typical facility range %	Uses	Disadvantages	Problems in writing
Multiple-choice: 3 option 4 option 5 option	33 25 20	Wide range 30 to 95	Recall, comprehension, application. Versatile		Enough good distractors needed
Multiple-response, 6 option. Student told to choose: 2 or 4 3 'more than 1'	6.7 5 1.8	Fairly difficult 10 to 70	Mainly recall and comprehension. Situations with several right and few wrong answers	Partial knowledge not rewarded	Clear distinction needed between right and wrong answers
Assertion/Reason, 5 option.	20	Usually rather difficult 20 to 75	Limited usefulness, mainly comprehension. Not for lower ability students		Questions must fit the standard options
Matching: no. of items in each list: 3 and 4 4 and 5	4 less than 1	Wide range 20 to 80	Limited usefulness, mainly recall	Partial knowledge not rewarded. Detailed analysis difficult	Lists must be homogeneous
True/false	50	Fairly easy 50 to 100	Limited usefulness. Mainly recall and comprehension		'Cue words' must be avoided. Larger number of questions needed to give the same reliability

(d) If more than one question type is used, questions of each type should be
     grouped together in the paper, so that students do not face unnecessary
     changes between question types.

(e) Writers who are not experienced are advised to concentrate initially on
     multiple-choice only.

(f) Mechanical marking systems are usually able to cope only with multiple-
     choice questions, or (if designed for five options) with multiple-choice
     and assertion/reason. Multiple-response and matching questions will
     probably need separate marking by hand. This ought not to be a factor in
     the choice if there are valid reasons for preferring questions of these
     types. If, however, there is no gain in validity from using matching or
     multiple-response questions, then it is more efficient to use only
     multiple-choice which can be marked mechanically.

(g) Questions of other types may be converted to a form of multiple-choice,
     suitable for machine marking, using the techniques described in Chapter
     8. These techniques should be used sparingly, however, as the end
     product is often a confusing question which tests mental agility more
     than knowledge of the subject matter.

APPLICATION

1. List the question types used in each objective exam or test with which
    you are concerned.

2. In each test, what is the most likely score for a student who guesses
    blindly?

3. Are there any tests containing only multiple-choice questions which
    would be improved if one or more other types were used as well?

4. Are any non-multiple-choice questions serving a useful purpose? Are
    they as well written as the multiple-choice questions?

5

Deciding the Examination Conditions

The 'examination conditions' include such matters as the number of questions to be asked, the time allowed and the material which may be used in the examination. Decisions on these points should be taken well in advance of the preparation of the first examination and normally when the syllabus itself is written, because:

(a) it is sensible to be sure, while the syllabus is still under discussion, that it can be tested validly and reliably;

(b) some decisions, such as those concerning the use of reference material and aids to calculations, affect the teaching of the course;

(c) students like to know in advance how they will be assessed—uncertainty leads to anxiety.

Once decided, the examination conditions should, if possible, remain unchanged for the life of the syllabus. Only if they are found to be seriously inappropriate should there be a major change during the life of the syllabus, as a change in the conditions may impair the reliability of the assessment.

In discussing the conditions we shall look first at the requirements of end-of-course or end-of-unit examinations and then consider what different factors affect the decisions concerning in-course tests.

There are nine points to be decided.

1. Type of Question and Number of Options

These have already been discussed (see Chapter 4).

2. Number of Questions

The number of questions in an objective examination should not normally exceed 100, as this is the likely limit of the student's concentration. For the lower ability levels (e.g. operative and part one craft) 80 is a more realistic limit. The theoretical reliability of the examination increases with the number of questions; a smaller number of questions covers a smaller proportion of the syllabus and increases the chances of 'freak' results due to successful guessing. The number of questions should not therefore normally be less than 50. It should be noted, however, that they must all be good questions. Increasing the number of questions by adding ten or 20 poor ones does nothing to improve the examination's reliability—it is much more likely to reduce reliability.

Within these limits—maximum 100 (80 for lower levels) and minimum 50—the number of questions used may depend to some extent on the amount of syllabus matter to be covered.

3. Time Allowed

The time allowed should be adequate for the number of questions to be answered. It is not usually an aim of the examinations to test speed of working and shortage of time tends to encourage guessing. The generally quoted time allowance of one minute per question is often found to be excessive unless the questions are particularly long and complex or include multiple-response or matching questions. However, in addition to the time actually needed for answering the questions, some time should be allowed for 'settling down' and some for students to check through their answers at the end. The following time allowances should be adequate:

Number of questions	Simple questions	Long or complex questions
50—60	1 hour	1 h 15 min
80	1 h 30 min	1 h 45 min
100	1 h 45 min	2 h

After the first one or two examinations the time allowance should be reviewed. Students may be asked to indicate how long they took and whether they had in fact finished at the end of the time period, and answer sheets may be checked to see how many students omitted the questions at the end. If it seems that more than a few students failed to finish comfortably in the time allowed, then the allowance should be increased.

A more common problem is that students faced with 80 or 100 questions feel rushed and work too quickly, often finishing well within the permitted time but failing to recheck their work at the end. Students should be advised (preferably both orally and on the paper) that the time allowed is quite adequate and should be given practice in answering objective questions to give them confidence. It also helps students' confidence if the questions at the beginning of the paper are relatively easy and quick to answer.

4. Questions Compulsory or Optional?

The normal practice of making all questions compulsory in an objective paper has the advantages that all students answer questions of the same difficulty and on the same syllabus sections. In a paper of long essays or other constructed-answer questions, a student would be excessively penalised if there happened to be a compulsory question on a part of the syllabus which he had not been taught or which, for example, he had missed through illness; this argument does not apply to objective questions, where each question is only a small part of the whole paper and where syllabus coverage is good. The normal rule should therefore be to make all questions compulsory.

The only exception to this rule is where the syllabus itself contains options. In this case, if it is decided to test everything in one paper, there should be a section of compulsory questions, covering the common section of the syllabus, and then two or more optional sections, covering the options in the syllabus. Within each section all questions should be compulsory so that, for example, a student who has studied Section B of the syllabus must answer all the Section B questions in the examination. Normally, the certificate or other award should indicate the option taken.

5. Aids to Calculation

'Aids to calculation' include logarithmic tables, slide rules and electronic calculators. Such aids are not strictly necessary in an objective paper, as the calculations are usually short and use easy figures. However, their use may be permitted if the student can be expected to make use of them in his occupation. Some restrictions on the use of electronic calculators may be necessary—for example that they be battery-operated and silent in operation.

If it is a specific aim of the course that the students be able to perform simple calculations without any aids, then it follows that no aids to calculation can be permitted in the examination. Students must be made aware of this from the beginning of the course.

In some courses the nature of the subject matter makes it necessary for students to have such tables as sines and cosines available in the examination. This would be obvious from the syllabus and the decision to involve such tables in the examination should be made at the beginning of the course.

6. Use of Reference Material

Permitting the use of specified reference material in the examination, which is sometimes of considerable benefit in constructed-answer examinations, is not usually a good idea for objective examinations. Questions testing the students' ability simply to look up facts in the reference works are of little value. The main use of reference material in an examination is to provide the source material to help the student in devising solutions to the problems given in the questions. This is most likely to be needed in long problem-solving or project-type questions which are unsuitable for conversion to objective questions and for which, indeed, there may be no single correct solution. There may, however, be some situations in which it is appropriate to allow or require the use of specified reference material in an objective examination. Travel time-tables and the *Tables of Current Rating and Voltage Drop of Conductors and Cables* for electrical installation students are examples of material which may be appropriate.

The use of reference material may be considered if:

(a) the reference material is familiar to the student and used either in his work or (as with specially prepared data sheets) in the course;

(b) the reference material is readily available, either owned by the student or supplied by the college;

(c) the reference works contain information which the student cannot be expected to memorise, but with which he should be familiar;

(d) the information is such that the student should be expected to apply it in his work;

(e) suitable objective questions can be set to test the students' application of the information.

7. Use of Separate Answer Sheets

Mechanical marking systems almost always require the student to mark his answers to the questions on a separate answer sheet which can be fed into the machine. This is more difficult for the student than marking his answers next to the question—it takes slightly longer and there is a danger of 'slipping', marking the answer to Question 7 in the space for Question 8 and so on. Students should be warned to check their answers and should be given the opportunity to practise using answer sheets of the type they will meet in their examination. With practice students should not find the use of a separate answer sheet too great a disadvantage.

If answers are to be marked manually, it is still easier for the marker if a separate answer sheet is used; there are fewer pages to turn and a template can be made to assist marking. However, because a separate answer sheet is more difficult for the student, it should probably be avoided for the lowest levels of the course or if the number of students is too small for the saving in marking time to be significant. If the paper includes multiple-response or matching questions a special answer sheet will be required; otherwise it is possible to use a standard pattern, valid for all courses and all papers.

8. Method of Scoring

The method of scoring should be to award one mark for each question correctly answered; this includes multiple-response or matching questions which are answered completely correctly. No credit is given for partly correct answers to such questions.

The temptation to award double marks for difficult questions or important topics or to award half marks for nearly right answers should be avoided. Differential weightings for questions cause complications in the scoring and determination of results without giving any clear advantages in validity or reliability. The specification can give appropriate weighting to important topics by requiring more questions on them.

9. A Correction for Guessing?

Some authorities recommend correcting each student's score to compensate for guessing, by using a formula such as the following:

$$S = R - \frac{W}{n - 1}$$

where

S is the corrected score,

R is the number of questions answered correctly,

W is the number of questions answered wrongly and

n is the number of possible answers.

For a four-option multiple-choice question, n is 4 and $(n - 1)$ is 3.

The assumption underlying this formula is that the student who has guessed on questions he did not know will have got one quarter of them right (if they are four-option questions) and three-quarters wrong; the number of wrong answers is therefore 3/4 the number on which he guessed.

Making a correction of this sort has two main aims:

(a) to cancel the advantage which the guesser obtained as compared with the more cautious student who simply omitted questions he did not know;

(b) to discourage students from guessing, since they are told in advance that guessing will be penalised.

However, the correction is of dubious value because:

(a) there is evidence that applying the correction has very little effect on the rank order of the students, although it depresses the marks of all;

(b) even if students know that a correction will be applied, the more adventurous will guess more freely than others;

(c) the correction can do nothing about the fact that some students will be more fortunate in their guesses than others;

(d) the marker cannot know that a wrong answer is the result of a 'guess'; it may well have been the confident choice of a well-worded distractor;

(e) blind guessing on more than a few questions is rare, particularly if the time allowed is adequate. Rather than guess blindly, students are likely to use what knowledge they have to eliminate one or two of the distractors, and then make an informed guess between the two or three options which remain;

(*f*) in the unlikely instance of a student guessing blindly on all the questions, he would almost certainly score well below the pass mark and so need not cause concern.

In general, any advantages to be gained by applying a guessing correction are outweighed by the extra work and complications involved, and it is better to score in a straightforward manner but to recognise that a small proportion of each student's score results from informed guessing.

Examination Conditions for In-course Tests

In-course tests are a series of tests which are taken at intervals during the course, each syllabus topic being tested immediately after it has been taught. There may be a short final test ranging over the whole syllabus and relating knowledge from different syllabus sections, but the series of in-course tests replaces a longer end-of-course or end-of-unit examination.

Results for the series of tests are usually aggregated so as to give the degree of reliability associated with a single, longer examination, but students who fail a test may be required to revise the subject matter and retake a similar test before proceeding.

The number of tests set will depend on the length of the course and the number of parts into which the syllabus matter can conveniently be divided. A suitable number of tests for a 240-hour, one-year course would be six to nine, depending partly on whether there were other assessment components. A series of four tests would normally be sufficient for a 60-hour unit.

Half an hour is an adequate length for each of the tests, the number of questions being 20—25. Other aspects of the examination conditions for in-course tests may be determined following the recommendations given for end-of-course examinations.

APPLICATION
Review the examination conditions for an objective examination or series of tests with which you are concerned.

1. Do the time allowance and number of questions conform to the recommendations of this chapter?

2. Is there evidence that the time allowance is suitable? If not, could such evidence be obtained?

3. Are all questions compulsory? If not, why not?

4. Are any aids to calculation or reference material allowed? Are they used?

5. Is a separate answer sheet used? Are the students given enough advice and practice to enable them to cope with it?

6. Is any complicated scoring system or guessing correction used? Is there any clear advantage for such a system?

6

Devising the Specification

A specification, such as that shown in Example 6.1, determines the number of questions to be set to test each syllabus topic and each ability in any one paper. The specification should be drafted well in advance of the first examination or pretest, preferably when the syllabus itself is being drafted. The attempt to draft a specification may reveal unexpected deficiencies in the syllabus itself, such as an undue emphasis on factual recall.

Once prepared, the specification should, if possible, remain unchanged for a number of years, preferably for the life of the syllabus. Sometimes, however, it may be found after the first one or two examinations that the specification is unsatisfactory or unworkable, and it must then be changed; this is most likely to occur if the writers have no previous experience of specifications.

EXAMPLES

6.1 *Specification for Multiple-choice Paper in Soft Furnishing*

| Topic | Number of questions testing | | | |
	Recall	Comprehension	Application	Total
Relation of articles to setting	3	2	5	10
Design	2	4	4	10
Equipment	2	—	2	4
Work study	2	3	5	10
Materials	4	2	4	10
Estimating	—	2	1	3
History	2	—	1	3
Total	15	13	22	50

Why Use a Specification?

The main reasons for using a specification are:

(a) to ensure that the weighting given to each topic in each examination is appropriate, so that there is not an undue emphasis on one topic or a neglect of an important aspect of the course; this contributes to the validity of the examination;

(b) to ensure that the abilities tested are appropriate and appropriately weighted, for example that there are sufficient questions requiring understanding and application; this also contributes to validity;

(c) to ensure that the weighting of topics and abilities is consistent from year to year; this contributes to the examination's reliability.

Weighting for Topics

When drafting a specification, it is best to divide the syllabus topics into from five to ten sections, according to the natural division of the subject matter. A specification with fewer than five topic sections would be insufficiently precise to give adequate control and consistency. One with more than ten or, at most 12, sections would be too detailed to be workable.

The number of questions allocated to each topic should be in proportion to its importance and to the teaching time devoted to it. However, some basic topics which are a necessary preliminary to the rest of the course may be given little or no separate weighting, as they are tested incidentally in the assessment of the other topics of the course.

In practice it may be found that some perfectly good questions relate to more than one syllabus topic and may be written and stored under either heading. Those compiling the paper need to be aware of this possibility and to avoid including in one paper two very similar questions which happen to have been allocated to different topics. If possible a consistent method of treating such questions should be adopted.

Abilities Tested

As already stated (see Chapter 1), the abilities most usually assessed in an objective paper are those of recall of facts (or 'information'), comprehension and application.

A *recall of facts* question requires the students to do no more than remember information which he has been taught. Examples 6.2 and 6.3 show questions testing recall; Example 6.2· requires the student simply to remember one of the constituents of piping chocolate; Example 6.3 requires him or her to identify a cleaning job which calls for the use of a strongly alkaline detergent.

A *comprehension* question involves something a little deeper; the student is required to show understanding of what he has been taught. Often, as in Examples 6.4 and 6.5, the question asks 'why?' and relates to the reasons for correct practice. Sometimes, comprehension questions test understanding of terms, conventions and diagrams and may require the conversion of information from one means of presentation to another (e.g. from verbal to diagrammatic or from graphical to calculation) in order to demonstrate understanding.

EXAMPLES

6.2 *Flour Confectionary*

Piping chocolate is made by blending melted chocolate with:
(a) glycerine
(b) fondant
(c) glucose
(d) cocoa butter.

6.3 *Housekeeping*

For which one of the following tasks should a strongly alkaline detergent be used?
(a) removing a build up of emulsion polish
(b) washing up crockery and cutlery
(c) laundering clothes
(d) damp dusting.

6.4 *Construction Technicians*

Honeycomb sleeper walls are used instead of solid brick sleeper walls in order to:
(a) decrease the number of bricks
(b) allow a free flow of air between ground floors
(c) impose less weight on the site concrete
(d) use up second quality bricks.

6.5 *Footwear Manufacture*

The usual reason for a zig-zag seam being used in stitching upper sections together is that it:
(a) lies flat
(b) is quicker to stitch
(c) is strong
(d) looks attractive.

In an *application* question, the student is required to go a little further and use his knowledge and understanding to solve a problem which is new to him. It should be noted that the problem or situation need not be new to the lecturer. In Example 6.6 the student is asked to use his knowledge of the construction of flash units to suggest the most likely cause of the fault described. In Example 6.7 he is required to apply his understanding of tension in overhead power lines and the effects of temperature to state what will happen in the given situation.

These abilities are a hierarchy, each involving those below it to some degree, so that comprehension questions generally require some measure of factual recall also, and application questions usually require that the student remembers and understands the information which he is asked to apply. It is sometimes difficult to decide to which category a particular question should be allocated. This is particularly true of application questions since a question which is application to one student may be factual recall to another who has already encountered the same problem. However, it is important to make the attempt, otherwise the paper is likely to be heavily weighted with recall questions which are easier to set.

It is easier to prepare the specification and to allocate questions to their ability categories if the syllabus is written in terms of examination objectives which state what the student is expected to be able to do by the end of the course.

EXAMPLES

6.6 *Photography*

The test lamp in the bulb circuit of a battery capacitor flash unit fails to operate. Replacing the bulb fails to cure the fault. When a bulb is removed and the electrical contacts in the socket are shorted together the test lamp still fails to function. The probable cause is:

(a)   poor contact between the socket and the bulb
(b)   that the battery is exhausted
(c)   that the shutter contacts are dirty
(d)   a break in the synchronisation lead.

6.7 *Power Lines and Cables*

A line is strung to its maximum allowable tension during erection on a warm day. If during the night the temperature falls, the effect on the conductor will be that:

(a)   its height is reduced
(b)   its height is increased
(c)   it is understressed
(d)   it is overstressed.

Calculations

It is sometimes found helpful to have a separate column for calculations in the specification. Usually, however, calculations may be included amongst the questions testing application. Transposition of formulae and substitution in formulae would be classed under comprehension.

For papers which contain a relatively large proportion of topics requiring calculations, it is wise to set a limit on the number of calculations which may be set in any one paper, so as to ensure that the paper is not over-burdened with them. Calculations are often easier to set than other objective questions, but may be less valuable, as they may relate less to the student's knowledge of the technology. Frequently calculations can be tested almost equally well by means of a constructed-answer paper, whereas the value of an objective paper lies in its ability to test understanding and application of the technical content of the course without asking the student to express himself at length in prose.

Drafting the Specification

The layout of the specification or 'grid' is usually as shown in Example 6.1. Another example is given as Example 6.8.

It is assumed that the total number of questions to be set has already been decided (see Chapter 5). The next stage is to decide the allocation of questions to each syllabus topic, adjusting them as necessary to give the required total. This gives the figures in the right-hand column. The number of questions to be set on each ability for each topic must then be determined; this gives the figures in each 'cell' of the grid. It is not, of course, necessary to set questions for each ability on each topic if they are not appropriate. In Example 6.8 no application questions are considered necessary on boiler work. Nor is it necessary for the proportion of comprehension or application questions to be the same for each topic. In Example 6.8 only one of the seven questions on cutting tests application, but two of the four questions on layout and planning test application—in the latter topic the student is more likely to be required to think and plan for himself.

When each cell has been completed the totals at the bottom are found, showing the overall balance between recall, comprehension and application. If the balance is not appropriate for the course in question, the figures in the individual cells must be reviewed and adjusted as necessary.

The balance shown in Example 6.8—16 questions on recall, 19 on comprehension and 15 on application—is a reasonable one for a more technical craft course at Part II level. An operative course or a less technical craft course might have a lower proportion of application questions—this will be seen in Example 6.9. Although it is often necessary, particularly when writing the questions, to beware of setting too many recall questions, an excess of application questions would be equally undesirable; the proportions must be appropriate for the level and nature of the course being tested, and there should not be an artificial attempt to set application questions where they are not relevant to the students' requirements.

A technician examination, however, should normally have a greater proportion of application questions than a craft examination, perhaps up to 50% in the first one or two years of the course. Later in the course the proportion of application and synthesis would be higher but would probably be assessed partly or entirely by constructed-answer questions or projects.

EXAMPLE

6.8   *Specification for Multiple-choice Paper in Structural and Thick Plate Craft*

Topic		Number of questions testing		
	Recall	Comprehension	Application	Total
Safety	1	1	1	3
Materials	1	2	1	4
Layout and planning of work	1	1	2	4
Cutting of sections of thick plate	3	3	1	7
Forming	2	2	2	6
Welding	1	2	1	4
Riveting and bolting	1	1	1	3
Boiler work	1	1	—	2
Assembly and erection	1	1	1	3
Surface protection	1	1	1	3
Associated studies	3	4	4	11
Total	16	19	15	50

EXAMPLE

6.9 *Specification for Series of In-course Tests in Basic Cookery*

Topic	Number of questions testing				
	Recall	Comprehension	Application	Total	
Test 1					
Safety	2	2	0	4	
Hygiene	2	4	2	8	
Use of cooking tools	4	3	1	8	
					20
Test 2					
Kitchen equipment	4	3	1	8	
Heat and fuels	3	2	1	6	
Working methods	1	1	1	3	
Salads	1	1	1	3	
					20
Test 3					
Commodities	2	2	1	5	
Stocks, sauces, gravies and soups	8	5	2	15	
					20
Test 4					
Fish	5	4	1	10	
Potatoes and vegetables	5	3	2	10	
					20
Test 5					
Meat and poultry	8	8	4	20	
					20
Test 6					
Eggs	4	3	1	8	
Farinaceous	3	2	1	6	
Breakfast dishes, snacks and sandwiches	3	2	1	6	
					20
Test 7					
Puddings, sweets and cakes	5	4	1	10	
Beverages	3	2	0	5	
Calculations	0	2	3	5	
					20
Test 8					
Safety and hygiene	1	2	1	4	
Nutrition	4	4	2	10	
Menus	2	2	2	6	
					20
Totals	70	61	29		160

The Specification for In-course Tests

Example 6.9 shows how a specification may be devised for a series of in-course tests. In this case there are eight tests, each containing 20 items.

The number of topics separately identified may be larger than for a single end-of-course examination and some topics (such as Safety and Hygiene in this example) may need to appear in more than one of the tests.

It is not always necessary for the tests to be taken in exactly the order shown. In Example 6.9 the order of Tests 3—7 could be varied to suit circumstances.

It should be noted that it is considered appropriate to have a larger percentage of recall questions and a smaller proportion of application in Cookery than in the Soft Furnishing and Structural and Thick Plate examples given earlier in the chapter.

APPLICATION
1. Review the specification for (*i*) an examination and (*ii*) a series of in-course tests with which you are concerned.
    (*a*) Is each specification divided into a workable number of syllabus topics?
    (*b*) Do the proportions of recall, comprehension and application questions conform to the recommendations of this chapter? If not, why not?
    (*c*) Are the specifications followed in practice?

2. (*a*) Draft a specification for an examination or series of tests which does not at present have one. Ask a colleague to comment on it.
    (*b*) How would the use of this specification improve the validity and reliability of the examination or tests?

PART III

Producing the Test

7

Basic Multiple-choice Question Writing

With the examination conditions and the specification determined, the lecturer or examiner is now ready to begin writing some questions—not as easy as it might at first sight appear. Writing multiple-choice questions requires a thorough knowledge of the subject matter, the course and the students and of the techniques of question writing. This chapter describes and illustrates the basic rules of multiple-choice question writing. Chapter 8 deals with the writing of multiple-response, assertion/reason and matching questions and their conversion to multiple-choice form. Chapter 9 considers some more sophisticated question-writing techniques for multiple-choice.

The question writer should not attempt to work in isolation; in order to improve his or her questions and expertise in writing them he or she needs the advice and constructive criticism of a colleague who is (if possible) equally conversant with the subject, the course, the students and the techniques involved. Sometimes it may be possible for writers to work together in a group of three or four, drafting questions together as a team. In other circumstances it may be better for one writer to prepare a draft and submit it to his colleague(s) for comment.

Questions should be written in accordance with the specification which shows the number of questions needed on each topic and ability for each examination or pretest. It is generally advisable to try to cover one topic at a time and to write most, if not all, of the questions on one topic before going on to the next. In any case, questions should be filed according to topic, so as to ensure that two similar or overlapping questions are not written.

Some authorities have recommended that in the first draft the key to each question should be (a), but this has considerable disadvantages:

(*a*) There is a danger of forgetting to change the questions, and finding one-self with a pretest or examination in which the answer to every question is (a).

(b) The need to rearrange every question is an extra chore which can lead to errors, particularly in the recording of the keys.

(c) Some questions require their options to be in a particular order (see Examples 7.25, 7.43, 7.44).

(d) It is best if the editor is not told at first which option is intended to be the key; he should make his own choice and only then look at the list of keys supplied by the writer (see Chapter 10 on editing).

It is therefore better if the keys are distributed in a random order as the questions are written; a pack of playing cards can be used to assist in this. Writers should beware of a tendency to put the key in the same place each time; some writers, in the attempt to avoid (a), make all their keys (b) or (c).

The basic rules of multiple-choice question writing which should be observed are set out below:

1. The Topic must be within the Syllabus and Specification

This is an obvious point, but one which is occasionally overlooked. In particular, it should be noted that a topic which is in the syllabus may not be in the specification if it is to be assessed in some other examination component. There is also no point in writing, for instance, an application question on boiler work, if the specification calls for only recall and comprehension questions on that topic (as in Example 6.8).

Interpretations of the syllabus may vary, particularly if it is not written in terms of examination objectives, and one of the purposes of editing (see Chapter 10) is to confirm that the question accords with a reasonable interpretation of the syllabus.

The syllabus section and the type of ability being assessed should be marked on the draft submitted to the editor.

2. The Topic must be a Worthwhile One

Not every topic which is within the syllabus merits a question. Questions should not be trivial, based on jargon, based on abstruse facts, too easy, too difficult or unrealistic.

Example 7.1 is a rather trivial question; the first clause of the stem gives a clear hint as to the answer. A more valuable question on the same topic would be Example 7.2.

Example 7.3 is a rather pointless test of knowledge of jargon, arguably outside the syllabus anyway. A question based on abstruse or irrelevant knowledge would also be unacceptable.

Example 7.4 is another question of dubious value, because the answer is rather obvious. In this case, because it is important that questions on safety should be asked, there may be a case for its inclusion, although an improved version would be preferable.

EXAMPLES

7.1 Cookery

A chef's clothing is designed for specific reasons; therefore coats should be worn with sleeves:

(a)   rolled up completely
(b)   partly turned up
(c)   at full length
(d)   omitted from the garment.

7.2 Cookery

Chefs' coats are made with long sleeves primarily to ensure that:

(a)   the wearer's other garments are protected from heat
(b)   watches and bracelets do not contact food
(c)   the wearer's other garments are protected from food splashes
(d)   the arms are protected from excessive heat.

7.3 Further Education Teachers

The term used to describe the language of students with limited verbal ability is:

(a)   restricted code
(b)   limited code
(c)   language deprivation
(d)   speech difficulties.

7.4 Foundry Craft

The regulations contained in Factory Acts are enforceable by law:

(a)   in all cases
(b)   never
(c)   if considered practicable by the worker
(d)   only if considered practicable by the employer.

Questions which are too difficult are also unacceptable, if they are based on knowledge which it is unreasonable to expect the student to remember. Questions which may come into this category are those which require recall of details of regulations or codes of practice, constants or complex formulae, exact doses of drugs, and so on. In some instances, where it is desirable to assess the student's use of information, it may be better to give the necessary information in the question (see Paragraph 5).

Example 7.5, although probably acceptable, could be argued to be unrealistic. The waiter is unlikely to find himself pacing the restaurant with a teaspoon looking for someone to whom to give it. A more practical question would be to ask what cutlery should be given to a customer who has ordered an avocado pear.

Calculation questions should normally be related to a practical example and should use realistic figures. Example 7.6 is preferable to a question which simply asks the student to subtract 1 from 2.40 and would also be preferable to one using impossible figures. However, the practical value of the question is open to doubt.

3. The Question should Test Relevant Abilities

Questions which test recall are usually much easier to write than those which test comprehension or application. However, the writer who is following the specification is obliged to attempt to produce comprehension and application questions, and these are frequently more valuable and more searching.

EXAMPLES

7.5 *Food Service*

A teaspoon is the correct piece of cutlery to give the customer for:
(a)   gnocchi parisienne
(b)   oeuf à la neige
(c)   fresh fruit salad
(d)   avocado pear.

7.6 *Motor Vehicle Craft*

A vehicle has a wheel base which is a metre longer than the track. If the wheel base is 2.40m, the track is:
(a)   1.40m
(b)   2.30m
(c)   2.50m
(d)   3.40m

4. The Question should not Require Irrelevant Abilities

A question which is intended to assess knowledge of the course subject matter should not be so designed that it can only be answered by students with above-average ability in reading comprehension, calculation or mental agility if these abilities are irrelevant to the course. Questions designed to test these abilities are admissible, indeed essential, if it is an express aim of the assessment to test such abilities. They should not, however, be used to test technical understanding as they will give a false impression of the students' knowledge.

Example 7.7 is a test of semantics rather than of subject knowledge. It is arguable whether there is a correct answer.

Example 7.8 is as much a test of mental agility as of knowledge of the properties of metals. It would be better asked as two straightforward multiple-choice questions, as in Examples 7.9 and 7.10, although they should probably not both appear in the same paper.

===

EXAMPLES

7.7 *Further Education Teachers*

Which one of the following statements is true?
(a)   Judgment cannot be made without discrimination.
(b)   Discrimination cannot be made without judgment.
(c)   Judgment and discrimination are different words to describe the same thing.
(d)   Discrimination is the opposite of judgment.

7.8 *Mechanical Engineering Craft*

List 1 Properties	List 2 Alloying element
(A) corrosion resistance	(P) lead
(B) hardness and toughness	(Q) chromium
(C) hot hardness	(R) vanadium
(D) ease of machining	(S) tungsten

Refer to the two lists above. Which of the following options shows correctly the main property of high speed steel and the alloying element which produces that property?

	Property	Alloying element
(a)	B	Q
(b)	C	R
(c)	D	S
(d)	C	S

Example 7.11 involves unnecessarily complex figures for a question intended to test knowledge of parallel resistors. To find the overall resistance R, students need to evaluate the expression:

$$\frac{1}{R} = \frac{1}{7} + \frac{1}{18} + \frac{1}{11}.$$

Simpler figures would test the relevant knowledge just as well.

EXAMPLES

7.9   *Mechanical Engineering Craft*

Which of the following is the most important property required of a high speed steel?
(a)   corrosion resistance
(b)   hardness and toughness
(c)   hot hardness
(d)   ease of machining.

7.10   *Mechanical Engineering Craft*

Which of the following alloying elements gives high speed steel its most important property?
(a)   lead
(b)   chromium
(c)   vanadium
(d)   tungsten.

7.11   *Electrical Craft*

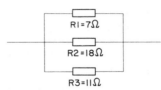

The combined resistance of the group of resistors shown in the above figure is:
(a) $2\,\Omega$
(b) $3.45\,\Omega$
(c) $12\,\Omega$
(d) $36\,\Omega$.

7.12   *Electrical Installation*

$Z = \sqrt{R^2 + X^2}$
If $R = 4$ and $X = 3$, the value of Z is:
(a) 5
(b) 7
(c) 25
(d) 49.

5. Provide any Necessary Information

Unless reference material is taken into the examination, the question should include any necessary information, formulae or constants which the student cannot be expected to remember. Alternatively this information may be given at the head of the paper.

In Example 7.12 the students are provided with the necessary formula. Students in a higher level of course would probably be expected to remember this formula.

It may be necessary to tell students what value of π to use (22/7 or 3.142).

6. Questions should not be Excessively Long

Some variation in the length and difficulty of the questions in the test is acceptable, but questions should not be excessively long. Example 7.13 requires the student to:

(a) perform nine multiplications to find the cost of, for example, two hors d'hœuvres;

(b) add the totals together with seven other items;

(c) find 12½% of the total and add it on.

This is excessive both for the length of time allowed for one question and for the single mark available. This question would be better asked in a constructed-answer paper.

A single question based on a complicated diagram or a passage of prose for comprehension may also be too long, but a group of several questions all based on a single diagram or passage would be acceptable (see the paragraph on question groups in Chapter 9, p.121).

7. The Stem should Pose the Question Clearly

The form of the stem may be either a question or an incomplete statement, but in any case it should make quite clear what is being asked. Normally, the bright student should have a good idea of what the expected answer is before reading the options.

Example 7.14 does not fulfil this requirement. Without reading the options the student does not know whether the question relates to the time for spraying, the equipment to be used, the type of chemical required, the type of crop for which it is most suitable or even the reasons for spraying. A better stem would be 'When should chemical weeding by spraying be carried out?'. Poorly worded stems often lead to poor options (see Paragraph 12).

8. Negative Stems should be Avoided or Emphasised

It is generally best to avoid negative stems if at all possible. They are often confusing and the student may, under the stress of examination nerves, fail to

---

EXAMPLES

7.13 *Food Service*

A customer's bill lists the following items:

2	hors d'oeuvres variés	@ £1.25
1	avocado vinaigrette	@ .95
2	moules marinières	@ £1.45
1	Florida cocktail	@ .75
2	darne de saumon	@ £2.45
1	chicken Maryland	@ £2.10
1	caneton bigarade	@ £2.40
2	entrecôte bordelaise	@ £2.85
2	salads	@ .60
2	cherry flans	@ .95
3	strawberries and cream	@ .85
1	gâteau	@ .70
6	coffees	@ .35
6	sherries	@ .55
1 × 17		@ £3.90
1 × 29		@ £4.20

What is the total of the bill before VAT if the service charge is 12½%?
(a) £26.30
(b) £29.59
(c) £42.05
(d) £47.31.

7.14 *Forestry*

Chemical weeding by spraying is best carried out:
(a)   after heavy rain
(b)   during the dormant season
(c)   after a prolonged dry period
(d)   during conditions of little or no wind.

notice the negative word and answer as if for a positive question. A stem may be negative even without the use of the word 'not'. 'Never', 'nowhere' and 'unsatisfactory' are negative words, as is 'false' in Example 7.15.

Example 7.15 is particularly unsatisfactory because options (b), (c) and (d) are also negative statements, so that a double negative is involved. It would be better to ask a positive question such as Example 7.16.

However, Example 7.16 is still unsatisfactory because the question is not clearly posed in the stem. It would be better still to select one aspect of the topic and ask a direct question on it, as in Example 7.17.

If a negative stem is unavoidable, the negative word should be emphasised with capitals or italics, as in Example 7.18.

EXAMPLES

7.15 *Psychology*

Which of the following statements is false?
(a) The average intelligence quotient is 100.
(b) Intelligence does not change much during a person's life.
(c) Bright parents never have mentally handicapped children.
(d) Outstandingly intelligent children do not always appear intelligent at school.

7.16 *Psychology*

Which of the following is a true statement about intelligence?
(a) The average intelligence quotient is 100.
(b) Intelligence increases up to the age of about 40, then declines.
(c) Bright parents never have mentally handicapped children.
(d) Outstandingly intelligent children invariably do well at school.

7.17 *Psychology*

Which of the following is valid evidence that intelligence is at least partly hereditary?
(a) Bright parents never have mentally handicapped children.
(b) Children from better class homes do better in intelligence tests.
(c) Children moved from orphanages to foster homes improve their intelligence test scores.
(d) Identical twins are more alike in intelligence than fraternal twins.

7.18 *Electricity Sub-station Plant*

The transformer vector group which will NOT parallel with a star-delta transformer is:
(a) star-delta
(b) star-star
(c) delta-star
(d) star-interstar.

The stem of a question should never contain a double negative, as in Example 7.19. This should be reworded to 'Which type of coffee should be boiled during preparation?'.

9. The Question should be as Concise as Possible

Although all necessary information must be given in the question, it should not include any unnecessary verbiage to add to the amount of reading required of the student. The stem should not contain any irrelevant material, and the temptation to teach in the questions should be avoided if the purpose of the test is assessment.

Example 7.20 has an unnecessarily long stem; a sufficient stem would be 'Boeuf en daube provençal is made with cubes of beef and:'.

Questions can often be shortened considerably by putting common words into the stem instead of into each of the options. Example 7.21 could be rewritten as shown in Example 7.22.

EXAMPLES

7.19 *Food Service*

It is a general rule that coffee should not be boiled with the exception of:
(a)   cona coffee
(b)   café royale
(c)   Turkish coffee
(d)   Café Hag.

7.20 *Cookery*

Boeuf en daube provençal consists of two meats cubed and marinaded before cooking. One is beef, the other is:
(a)   lamb
(b)   pork
(c)   veal
(d)   mutton.

7.21 *Food Service*

The plate for asparagus should be:
(a)   placed flat on the table
(b)   supported under the right hand side by an inverted large fork
(c)   supported under the left hand side by an inverted large fork
(d)   supported under the top of the plate by an inverted large fork.

10. Diagrams should be Used where Appropriate

The use of a diagram can often make the question clearer and more concise. Example 7.23 would be very difficult to ask using words only. In many technical subjects diagrams are a natural medium of expression and students, particularly at the lower levels, have a greater facility in interpreting diagrams than in reading the written word. This is in accordance with the requirements of their employment.

11. The Key must be Correct

This is another obvious point which is not always observed. The key (or correct answer) must be technically correct, clearly preferable to the alternative answers provided, and not subject to dating, fashion or variations in local practice.

EXAMPLES

7.22 *Food Service*

The plate for asparagus should be supported by an inverted large fork placed under the:
(a)   right side
(b)   left side
(c)   top edge
(d)   bottom edge.

7.23 *Roadwork*

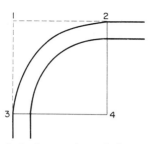

Which point in the above figure is the intersection point?
(a)   1
(b)   2
(c)   3
(d)   4 .

Example 7.24 is unacceptable because any of the answers could be true.

The answer to Example 7.25 would vary according to local practice and the preferences of the medical staff, so it is not a viable question.

The answer to Example 7.26 is so likely to change that it would not be wise to include it in a question paper or bank. In questions requiring students to calculate the VAT payable on an item it is wise to state in the question the rate of VAT to be applied.

If necessary, the authority for the statement should be given in the question, as in Example 7.27 where the relevant authority is the IEE Regulations.

EXAMPLES

7.24   *Further Education Teachers*

Other than for illness and working late, the most likely reason for irregular attendance of evening students is that:

(a)   they are falling behind with their work
(b)   they dislike the atmosphere of the class
(c)   the course does not seem clearly relevant to their job
(d)   the teacher does not give them much help.

7.25   *Nursing Studies*

Vaccination against measles is usually carried out at the age of:

(a)   6 months
(b)   9 months
(c)   1 year
(d)   2 years.

7.26   *Retail Distribution*

What is the current rate of VAT?

(a)   8%
(b)   12½%
(c)   15%
(d)   25%

7.27   *Electrical Installation*

According to the IEE Regulations, when is it compulsory to install a *switched* socket outlet?

(a)   when the supply is d.c.
(b)   when the supply is a.c.
(c)   for ring circuits
(d)   for radial circuits.

In Example 7.28 the key is a true statement, but not the most obvious answer to the question posed. Students would naturally expect the answer to this question to be concerned with the fact that the grapes are gathered late. In this instance the problem could best be overcome by rewording the stem to read 'One of the characteristics of "spätlesen" wines is that they:'.

It is not always necessary for the distractors to be completely wrong statements. It is acceptable to ask, as in Example 7.29, 'Which of the following is the most suitable . . .?' provided that subject experts are all agreed which of the options is the best.

12. The Options should all be Homogeneous

In any one question each of the options should be the same in form and nature; for example they might all be materials or circumstances or reasons. They should not be a 'ragbag' of dissimilar statements, as in Example 7.30. As already noted in Paragraph 7, poor stems often result in poor options. A better stem for Example 7.30 would be 'A function of the walls of the alveoli is to:', but this would require a new set of distractors.

EXAMPLES

7.28 *Alcoholic Beverages Service*

'Spätlesen' wines are wines which:
- (a) are estate-bottled
- (b) are sparkling
- (c) have had a controlled quantity of sugar added during fermentation
- (d) have had no sugar added during fermentation.

7.29 *Structural and Thick Plate Craft*

Which of the following processes would be most suitable for cleaning and resurfacing a steel bridge?
- (a) flame cleaning and painting
- (b) shot blasting and painting
- (c) wire brushing and metal spraying
- (d) cladding with protective sheeting.

7.30 *Nursing Studies*

The walls of the alveoli:
- (a) allow diffusion of gases
- (b) are capable of active contraction
- (c) are made of columnar epithelium
- (d) are in contact with the parietal pleura.

In Example 7.31 one of the options (d) is out of line with the rest. The question might perhaps be better recast with the use of a diagram, as in Example 7.23.

13. The Distractors must be Wrong but Plausible

We have already seen (Paragraph 11) that the key must be undeniably better than any of the distractors. The distractors should be not only wrong, but also fair for the level of student being tested. In Example 7.32 the intended key is (c), but (d) is sufficiently close to the truth to be arguably an unfair distractor for cookery students. 'Completely emulsify fats' would be slightly preferable. The distractors should not be so close as to mislead knowledgeable students.

The distractors must, however, be plausible so as to attract responses from those students who do not know the correct answer. They must not be silly, inherently implausible, ungrammatical, out of date or outside the syllabus.

EXAMPLES

7.31   *Sheet Metal and Thin Plate Craft*

When a radiused corner is being folded on a folding machine, the position of the reference line from which bending starts is:
(a)   on the folded side of the bend allowance
(b)   on the centre of the bend
(c)   on the gripped side of the bend allowance
(d)   scribed deeply to ensure bending starts at that point.

7.32   *Cookery*

Gastric juice is produced in a normal human stomach each day in order to:
(a)   break starch down into glucose
(b)   break proteins into their amino acids
(c)   partly break down protein intake
(d)   emulsify fats into their fatty acids.

7.33   *Horticulture*

A biennial plant is one which flowers:
(a)   every year
(b)   every other year
(c)   once only
(d)   in its second year and then dies.

In Example 7.33 neither (a) nor (c) is a plausible distractor, given the term 'biennial' in the stem; better would be '(a) twice in one year', '(c) twice and then dies'. None of the distractors in Example 7.34 is likely to be plausible to more than a handful of students.

In Example 7.35, (b) is not a plausible distractor and (a) is dubious. It would be better to turn the question round as shown in Example 7.36.

Options (a) and (c) in Example 7.37 are inherently implausible because one does not want grains of rice to cling together in groups or as a mass. Better distractors would be possible if the question read as in Example 7.38.

EXAMPLES

7.34   *Agriculture—Crops*

Trace elements are required by plants:
(a)   in large quantities
(b)   in small quantities
(c)   not at all
(d)   at certain times of the year.

7.35   *Basic Cookery*

In the process of canning foods the micro-organisms present in the food are:
(a)   partially destroyed
(b)   unaffected
(c)   retarded in growth
(d)   completely detroyed.

7.36   *Basic Cookery*

In which of the following methods of food preservation are the micro-organisms present in the food completely destroyed?
(a)   curing
(b)   freezing
(c)   drying
(d)   canning.

7.37   *Basic Cookery*

Rice is placed to cook in boiling salted water to ensure that the grains:
(a)   cling together in groups
(b)   remain entirely separate
(c)   join together as a mass
(d)   burst and break up.

Option (d) still does not sound very plausible, but was chosen by 8% of pretest students. This illustrates the point that the final judgment as to the acceptability of distractors should sometimes be left until after the question has been tried out. Distractors which seem suitable to the question writer and the editors may prove to be quite unattractive to students (or alternatively to mislead good students unfairly), while others may prove more distracting than expected. However, obviously silly distractors should be eliminated before pretest as it is a waste of resources to try them out.

Distractors are not plausible if they do not follow grammatically from the stem, as options (c) and (d) in Example 7.39.

There should be a logical reason for the distractors used in a calculation question. They should be the result of likely errors of method or calculation, not figures plucked out of thin air. This is discussed further in Chapter 9.

Distractors based on out-of-date information or on material which is outside the syllabus are unfair and should be excluded.

A distractor which is dissimilar in nature from the other distractors is likely to be implausible; option (d) in Example 7.31 is a case in point.

14. There should be no Clues

A question or test should not contain clues which lead the student to the correct answer even if he does not know it. Repetition in the key of important

EXAMPLES

7.38 *Basic Cookery*

Rice is placed to cook in boiling water to ensure that:
(a)   maximum flavour is retained
(b)   the grains remain entirely separate
(c)   cooking time is kept to a minimum
(d)   the grains burst and break up.

7.39 *Horticulture*

A group of similar plants all raised by vegetative means from the same parent plant is called a:
(a)   family
(b)   clone
(c)   order
(d)   cuttings.

words in the stem may provide such a clue. The inclusion of the words 'tucked in' in (a) of Example 7.40 is likely to lead students to select this option, whether or not they have the requisite knowledge.

A similar clue may be provided by the use of synonyms in the stem and key, such as 'tactile' and 'touch' in Example 7.41. However, the level of verbal ability required to appreciate a clue such as this may be higher than that possessed by the majority of the students taking the test.

Students may also be drawn to the key if it is markedly longer or more precise than the distractors, such as (c) in Example 7.42. They are particularly likely to use clues of this sort if the key is consistently longer than the distractors throughout the test.

Students may also notice, perhaps subconsciously, if the key is, for example, more often (b) than one of the alternatives. For this reason it is important to ensure that the keys are distributed randomly.

EXAMPLES

7.40 *Soft Furnishing*

The term 'tuck in' means:
(a)   extra material tucked in between chair back and seat
(b)   material used for extra strength round corners
(c)   a corner pleat
(d)   a gathered frill.

7.41 *Nursing Studies*

The function of a tactile corpuscle is to:
(a)   detect heat
(b)   respond to pain
(c)   detect touch
(d)   produce sweat.

7.42 *Furniture Craft*

The most important reason why a spray booth is fitted with 'anti-flash' lighting is because:
(a)   it casts no shadows
(b)   it is cheaper to install
(c)   it reduces the risk of explosion in conditions where there are evaporating solvents
(d)   bulb-changing is easier.

15. Options should not Overlap

Overlapping options should be avoided, as they may result in there being more than one correct answer. In Example 7.43 the intended key is (a), but (b) and (c) are also true—the specification should be drawn up before any items are requested and before the first pretest. These options should be reworded, so that (b) reads 'after completion of the syllabus but before items are requested' and (c) reads 'when items have been edited but before the first pretest'.

Overlapping options occur more frequently with numerical questions. In Example 7.44 the intended key is (c), but it is also true that the lintel should not be less than 500 mm (b) or even 400 mm (a). The stem should be reworded to 'The minimum permissible length of concrete lintel for a 350 mm fireplace opening is:', possibly with a reference to the regulations or code of practice concerned.

16. Avoid 'None of these' and 'All of these'

'None of these' is usually included, as in Example 7.45, because the writer cannot think of a third plausible distractor. It is not likely to be plausible itself, particularly if it occurs several times in the paper but is never the key. In general, it is best avoided. Chapter 9 (p.124) looks at ways of overcoming the problem of insufficient plausible distractors.

EXAMPLES

7.43 *Achievement Testing*

When should a test specification be drawn up?
(a)   while the syllabus is being prepared
(b)   before any items are requested
(c)   before the first pretest
(d)   when there are enough items in the bank.

7.44 *Brickwork*

The length of concrete lintel for a 350 mm fireplace opening should not be less than:
(a)   400 mm
(b)   500 mm
(c)   575 mm
(d)   750 mm.

'All of these' should not be used as a distractor or as the key. If, as in Example 7.46, 'all of these' is the key, then all the other options are also true. This question may be rewritten as shown in Example 7.47.

17. Use Preferred Terminology, Abbreviation and Units

The question should use correct preferred terminology, abbreviations and units. A helpful guide to S.I. units and abbreviations is the CTEB booklet *S.I. Symbols, Abbreviations and Conventions* published by City & Guilds of London Institute.

It should not be necessary to add that grammar and spelling should be correct. Particular pitfalls are proper names (of people or applied to their inventions) and foreign terms used, for example in cuisine and the service of wine. Trade names and jargon should be avoided if at all possible.

EXAMPLES

7.45 *Sheet Metal and Thin Plate Craft*

Which of the following is a permanently fastened joint?
(a) nut and bolt
(b) pop rivet
(c) rivet nut
(d) none of these.

7.46 *Science Laboratory Technicians*

Which of the following are properties of hydrogen chloride?
(a) not acidic when completely dry
(b) very soluble in water, producing acid
(c) a colourless choking gas
(d) all of these.

7.47 *Science Laboratory Technicians*

Which of the following are properties of hydrogen chloride?
1 not acidic when completely dry
2 very soluble in water, producing acid
3 a colourless choking gas.
(a) 1 only
(b) 1 and 2 only
(c) 2 and 3 only
(d) 1, 2 and 3.

18. Use a Logical and Consistent Order for the Options, where Applicable

Numerical options should be arranged consistently in ascending order of magnitude, as in Example 7.48, or if preferred, consistently in descending order throughout the test. The only exception is a question like Example 7.49.

There may be a logical order for options of other types. Those which relate to a sequence of operations, as Examples 7.43 and 7.50, should be arranged in correct order—unless, of course, the question asks which operation should be done first.

EXAMPLES

7.48   *Marine Electrical Plant*

An open-type switchboard is permitted for use on a.c. systems up to a maximum voltage of:
(a)   24 V
(b)   55 V
(c)   110 V
(d)   440 V.

7.49   *Electrical Craft*

Which of the following voltages is the largest?
(a)   1 V
(b)   1 kV
(c)   10 mV
(d)   10 V.

7.50   *Basic Cookery*

The correct stage at which to fold lightly whipped cream into a bavarois mixture is:
(a)   when creaming the egg yolks and sugar
(b)   before adding the gelatine to the sauce
(c)   immediately after the gelatine is added to the sauce
(d)   when the gelatine has almost set the mixture.

7.51   *Hairdressing*

What would you do immediately if a hairdresser burnt her hand?
(a)   plunge the hand into cold water
(b)   bathe the hand in warm water
(c)   apply petroleum jelly
(d)   apply a sterile dressing.

19. The Word 'You' should be Avoided

The word 'you' should be avoided if possible. A question which asks 'What would you do if . . .' allows the student to answer what he or she would actually do, not what is correct. The student's accurate answer to Example 7.51 might well be that she would 'apply petroleum jelly' or 'call an ambulance' or even 'scream and then faint'.

APPLICATION

1. Reexamine some questions which you have written or which appeared in a test with which you are concerned.

    (a) Does each fulfil all the criteria given in the chapter?

    (b) Rewrite any unsatisfactory questions.

2. If appropriate to your subject area, write some new questions as follows

    (a) one or more questions on 'difficult' areas of the syllabus;

    (b) a question providing information or data;

    (c) a question using a diagram;

    (d) a question quoting the authority for the answer;

    (e) a question asking 'Which of the following is best . . .?';

    (f) a question asking 'At which stage should . . . be done?'.

Ask a colleague to comment on your draft questions.

8

Preparing Other Types of Objective Question

Many of the principles of writing multiple-choice questions outlined in Chapter 7 apply equally to other types of objective question. In this chapter we look at some of the special considerations which apply when writing multiple-response, assertion/reason and matching questions.

We also look at ways in which these and true/false questions may be converted to a multiple-choice format. There are three main reasons why writers may wish to do this:

(a) to allow easier marking, particularly if some form of mechanical marking is to be used;

(b) to allow easier and more meaningful analysis (particularly for matching questions);

(c) to make the questions closer in level of difficulty to the multiple-choice items in the test.

Conversion of other types to the multiple-choice format can, however, make the questions over-complicated. They may appear to be testing higher abilities, while in fact emphasising irrelevant aspects of mental agility at the expense of understanding of the subject. Writers should guard against this danger.

The following points should be observed:

Writing Multiple-response Questions

(a) In any one test the number of options in the multiple-response questions should be fixed and should be more than in multiple-choice questions. Six is a suitable number. The number of correct answers may vary from question to question.

(b) It is generally best for the question to state how many answers are correct, as in Example 8.1. This is easier for the student, which is no bad thing in questions which tend to be more difficult than multiple-choice. It also helps to emphasise that this is not a multiple-choice question. In a test which includes multiple-response questions, the stems of the multiple-choice questions should (in appropriate cases,) read 'Which ONE of the following . . .'

(c) There should be a clear distinction between right and wrong answers. In Example 8.2 any answer, except cast iron, could be correct depending

---

EXAMPLES

8.1 *Fashion*

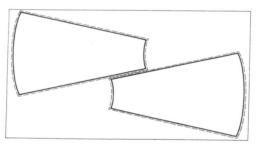

For which THREE of the following fabrics would the skirt pattern and layout shown in the above diagram be suitable?

(a) plain needlecord

(b) plain wool/cotton mixture

(c) wool/cotton mixture with a one-way design

(d) plain jersey

(e) worsted with small even checks

(f) striped cotton.

8.2 *Basic Engineering*

Which of the following metals may be forged easily?

(a) cast iron

(b) wrought iron

(c) low carbon steel

(d) high carbon steel

(e) aluminium alloys

(f) brass.

upon one's definition of 'easily'. Specifying the number of correct answers required, as in Example 8.3, may help, but if the distinction between right and wrong is a very fine one another form of question should be used.

(d) The options should be homogeneous, as for multiple-choice questions. Non-homogeneous options may give unintended clues, as in Example 8.4, where the student may well appreciate that the correct answers are (a), either (b) or (c), and one of (d), (e) and (f).

(e) Other clues should be avoided. For example, in Example 8.5 it is fairly obvious that the answers will be two adjacent values. The question could just as easily ask students to select one of four ranges of values, e.g. '60 to 80 mg/ml, 90 to 110 mg/ml'.

EXAMPLES

8.3 *Basic Engineering*

Which TWO of the following materials are most brittle?
(a)   high carbon steel
(b)   low carbon steel
(c)   aluminium
(d)   copper
(e)   cast iron
(f)   tin.

8.4 *Cookery/Food service*

Which THREE of the following should be served as accompaniments to smoked trout?
(a)   brown bread and butter
(b)   wedged lemon
(c)   sliced lemon
(d)   horseradish sauce
(e)   tartare sauce
(f)   mayonnaise sauce.

8.5 *Practical Nursing*

Which TWO of the following are normal fasting blood sugar levels?
(a)   70 mg   glucose/100 ml blood
(b)   90 mg   ″   ″   ″
(c)   110 mg   ″   ″   ″
(d)   130 mg   ″   ″   ″
(e)   150 mg   ″   ″   ″
(f)   170 mg   ″   ″

(*f*) It is not usually desirable to have all but one of the options correct, as in Example 8.6. This is in effect asking which one is wrong. Example 8.7 shows how this question could be revised to give four correct and two wrong answers.

Converting Multiple-response Questions to Multiple-choice

There are three ways in which a multiple-response question may be converted to multiple-choice.

(*a*) The number of options may be reduced so that there is only one key and the required number of distractors. Example 8.8 is a six-option multiple-

---

EXAMPLES

8.6 *Cookery*

Which FIVE of the following are ingredients of ratatouille?
(a) aubergine
(b) onion
(c) courgette
(d) marrow
(e) green pepper
(f) tomato.

8.7 *Cookery*

In addition to tomato, the FOUR ingredients of ratatouille are:
(a) aubergine
(b) onion
(c) courgette
(d) marrow
(e) green pepper
(f) chillies.

8.8 *Achievement Testing*

Which THREE of the following question types are objective?
(a) short-answer
(b) true/false
(c) completion
(d) matching
(e) structured
(f) assertion/reason.

response question, converted to four-option multiple-choice in Example 8.9. Example 8.9 is of course easier.

If the original question has four keys, as in Example 8.10, a new distractor must be found. In Example 8.11 a new distractor (d) has been produced by modifying a correct answer (f) of the original.

EXAMPLES

8.9   *Achievement Testing*

Which ONE of the following question types is objective?
(a)   short-answer
(b)   completion
(c)   structured
(d)   assertion/reason.

8.10   *Achievement Testing/Further Education Teachers*

Which FOUR of the following are correctly written examination objectives? (Each should be understood to be prefaced by 'At the end of the course the student should'):
(a)   understand why discharge stacks must be inside a building
(b)   list six metals which are elements
(c)   appreciate the importance of safe working methods
(d)   solve simple problems using Ohm's Law
(e)   state the ingredients of ratatouille
(f)   explain the principle of operation of a bimetal thermostat.

8.11   *Achievement Testing/Further Education Teachers*

Which of the following is a correctly written examination objective? (Each should be understood to be prefaced by the words 'At the end of the course the student should'):
(a)   understand why discharge stacks must be inside a building
(b)   appreciate the importance of safe working methods
(c)   solve simple problems using Ohm's Law
(d)   know the principle of operation of a bimetal thermostat.

8.12   *Cookery*

Which THREE of the following fruits are in season during June and July?
(a)   blackberries
(b)   cherries
(c)   damsons
(d)   raspberries
(e)   strawberries
(f)   satsumas.

(b) The student may be given a choice of four likely combinations of answers. Example 8.13 shows how this may be done testing the same knowledge as the multiple-response question in Example 8.12. The multiple-choice question is easier and may be particularly so if the combinations given in the options are not well chosen. The student may be able to identify the correct answer from only partial knowledge. In Example 8.13 the student who knows (as most of them will) that satsumas are not in season in June—July can eliminate options (a) and (d). If he also knows (as many will) that raspberries are in season then, he can be sure that the key is (c), whether or not he knows about blackberries, damsons, cherries and strawberries. The question would be improved if satsumas were removed and different combinations of the other five items used.

This method can only be used if the original options are quite short.

(c) If the options of the multiple-response question are longer, as in Example 8.14, it may be better to number them and make each of the options of the multiple-choice question a combination of numbers, as has been done in Example 8.15. This introduces an extra stage for the student, irrelevant to the testing of his subject knowledge and the method should therefore be used with reservation. It is probably not suitable for operative, part one craft and similar levels.

EXAMPLES

8.13 *Cookery*

In which ONE of the following options are all three fruits in season during June and July?
(a) blackberries, raspberries, satsumas
(b) blackberries, damsons, strawberries
(c) cherries, raspberries, strawberries
(d) cherries, damsons, satsumas.

8.14 *Cookery*

Which FOUR of the following are ingredients of the fish stuffing used in the preparation of paupiettes of fish?
(a) whiting fillet
(b) breadcrumbs soaked in milk
(c) dry mashed potato
(d) savoury choux paste
(e) white of eggs
(f) béchamel.

Like the previous method, this method of converting multiple-response to multiple-choice has the disadvantage that the student may be able to answer from only partial knowledge. Both for this reason and because of the complexity of the method, it may often be better to reduce the number of items in the list. More than enough combinations can be obtained if two items are to be chosen from four.

'Combination questions' such as these are discussed further in Chapter 9.

Writing Assertion/Reason Questions

Really good assertion/reason questions are exceptionally difficult to write.

(a) The options used should be standard throughout the test. Those shown in Example 8.16 may be varied provided that all the questions in any one test are consistent.

EXAMPLES

8.15 *Cookery*

Which of the ingredients listed below are used in the fish stuffing for paupiettes of fish?
(1) whiting fillet
(2) breadcrumbs soaked in milk
(3) dry mashed potato
(4) savoury choux paste
(5) white of eggs
(6) béchamel.

(a) 1, 2, 3, 5
(b) 1, 4, 5, 6
(c) 2, 3, 4, 5
(d) 2, 3, 5, 6.

8.16 *Carpentry and Joinery*

ASSERTION   REASON
Western red cedar is used for   BECAUSE   it is resistant to decay.
external boarding

With reference to the above assertion and reason, which of the following is correct?

(a) Both assertion and reason are true statements and the reason is a correct explanation of the assertion.
(b) Both assertion and reason are true statements, but the reason is not a correct explanation of the assertion.
(c) The assertion is true but the reason is a false statement.
(d) The assertion is false but the reason is a true statement.
(e) Both assertion and reason are false statements.

(*b*) It is normally best to write out the options in full for each question. Failure to do so is likely to lead to confusion. However, all questions of this type would normally appear together in the test and it may be acceptable—provided the students are familiar with the style—to use a matrix as shown in Examples 8.17 to 8.20. In this case all the questions should appear on the same or facing pages.

(*c*) Writers should resist the tendency to make the key always either (a) or (b). Option (e) should be used approximately as often as the others.

(*d*) All the options should ideally be plausible in each question. This is particularly difficult to achieve. Sometimes, as in Examples 8.19 and 8.21, it is fairly obvious that the assertion is a correct statement, so options (d) and (e) may be excluded. Sometimes, as in Examples 8.17 and 8.19, there is a link between the assertion and the reason which makes it unlikely that (b) could be the key.

EXAMPLES

8.17—8.20 *Cookery*

For EACH of Examples 8.17 to 8.20 decide which of the following is correct and mark the appropriate letter beside it.

(a) Both assertion and reason are true statements and the reason is a correct explanation of the assertion.

(b) Both assertion and reason are true statements, but the reason is not a correct explanation of the assertion.

(c) The assertion is true but the reason is a false statement.

(d) The assertion is false but the reason is a true statement.

(e) Both assertion and reason are false statements.

	ASSERTION		REASON	
8.17	A cooked roast joint is removed from the oven to set before service	BECAUSE	this makes carving easier.	(a)
8.18	A hard-boiled egg should be left to cool gradually before shelling	BECAUSE	hasty cooling causes a dark ring round the yolk.	(b)
8.19	When a Christmas pudding is to be flamed the plate must be hot	BECAUSE	this will allow the brandy to burn slowly, so that the waiter can serve it flaming.	(c)
8.20	Scrambled eggs may become watery	BECAUSE	the eggs used are stale.	(d)

(e) The reason should be a freestanding statement. In Examples 8.20 and 8.22 the reasons are not freestanding, but can be considered only in relation to the assertion. In these examples the word 'because' should more logically read 'if'. Questions of this sort are not suitable for the assertion/reason format. Example 8.23 is much better because both the assertion and the reason may be considered separately before the possible connection between them is examined.

(f) The question should not be ambiguous because of doubts as to whether the reason given is the main reason for the assertion. In Example 8.24 the assertion and the reason are both true statements, but the reason given is not the main reason for choosing a sheltered site (which concerns damage to young plants). However, students may perhaps see it as a possible

EXAMPLES

8.21   *Electrical Installation*

ASSERTION		REASON
Care must be taken when terminating mineral-insulated cable	BECAUSE	ingress of moisture destroys the insulating properties of the magnesium oxide.

With reference to the above assertion and reason, which of the following is correct? (Options as for Example 8.16.)

8.22   *Nursing Studies*

ASSERTION		REASON
Retrolental fibroplasia occurs in premature infants	BECAUSE	oxygen in excess of their physiological requirements is given.

With reference to the above assertion and reason, which of the following is correct? (Options as for Example 8.16.)

8.23   *Anatomy and Physiology*

ASSERTION		REASON
The right main bronchus is wider, shorter and more vertical than the left	BECAUSE	the heart lies a little to the left of the midline.

With reference to the above assertion and reason, which of the following is correct?: (Options as for Example 8.16.)

8.24   *Horticulture*

ASSERTION		REASON
A nursery site should be sheltered	BECAUSE	wind may spread unwanted seeds.

With reference to the above assertion and reason, which of the following is correct? (Options as for Example 8.16.)

contributory reason and be puzzled as to what answer is intended. In a case such as this pretesting would be desirable to establish whether or not the question did confuse the more knowledgeable students.

Converting Assertion/Reason Questions to Multiple-choice

If five-option multiple-choice questions are being used, there is no problem—the assertion/reason questions are compatible. If, as is more usual, four-option questions are used, the assertion/reason questions may be adapted to the same format by deleting the fifth option—ensuring, of course, that this is not the key.

EXAMPLE

8.25 *Embroidery*

Match the stitch names in the list below with the illustrations given.

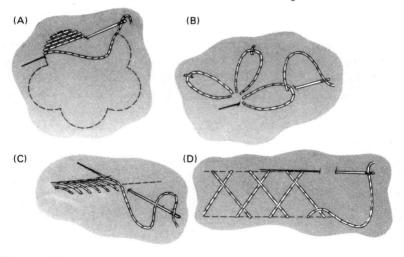

(A) (B) (C) (D)

(1) lazy daisy
(2) herringbone
(3) satin stitch
(4) chain stitch
(5) stem stitch

A	B	C	D

Writing Matching Questions

(a) A *match panel* should be provided as in Example 8.25 for the students to use in answering the question.

(b) The number of items in each list should be consistent in any one test. As in Example 8.25, it is usually best to have one more item in List 2 than in List 1. It is not then possible to answer the last item by elimination.

(c) The usual rule is for each item in List 2 to be used only once, and this is generally preferable. If it is decided for any particular reason that the matching should not be on a one-to-one basis, the stem must state this, as in Example 8.26.

(d) The items in each list should be homogeneous, so that the basis for the matching is the same throughout the question. In Example 8.27 there is no good reason why items (4) and (5) should not read 'vitamin C' and 'vitamin B complex'.

(e) Each of the items in List 2 should, if possible, be a plausible distractor for *each* of the items in List 1, and obvious pairings should be avoided. This is often difficult to achieve. In Example 8.28 the pairing of 'tomatoes' with 'fruit' is rather obvious and the question would be improved if some other example could be found—possibly a less well known vegetable such as aubergine.

(f) The questions should not contain clues as to the correct pairings. Example 8.29, which is a question of dubious value anyway, contains grammatical clues to lead the student to the correct answer, whatever his

---

EXAMPLE

8.26 *Alcoholic Beverages Service*

Match the wines in List 1 with the countries of origin in List 2. (Each item in List 2 may be used once, more than once or not at all.)

List 1	List 2
(A) Vouvray	(1) Germany
(B) Johannisberger	(2) Portugal
(C) Soave	(3) France
(D) Tavel	(4) Yugoslavia
	(5) Italy

A	B	C	D

EXAMPLES

8.27 *Cookery/Food and Family*

Match the foodstuffs in List 1 with the nutrients of which they are a good source in List 2.

List 1
(A) animal fats
(B) wholemeal flour
(C) citrus fruits
(D) vegetable oils

List 2
(1) vitamin A
(2) vitamin E
(3) vitamin K
(4) ascorbic acid
(5) riboflavine

A	B	C	D

8.28 *Cookery/Food and Family*

Match the vegetables in List 1 with their classification in List 2.

List 1
(A) leeks
(B) potatoes
(C) swedes
(D) tomatoes

List 2
(1) fruit
(2) root
(3) tuber
(4) flower
(5) bulb

A	B	C	D

8.29 *Further Education Teachers*

Match the descriptions in List 1 with the terms in List 2.

List 1
(A) The general studies lecturer assembles eight students to discuss delinquency. They form
(B) After some time another student joins them but is resented. He is part of
(C) A member of the original group is blamed by the others when discussion falters. He is made
(D) A member who initially argued against the others is won over. He has adopted

List 2
(1) the outgroup
(2) the scapegoat
(3) the group morale
(4) a face to face group
(5) the group norm.

A	B	C	D

knowledge of the terms. For example, (A) in List 1 is the item most likely to be followed by the indefinite article; (C) could hardly be followed by a type of group.

(g) Writers should ensure that Item (5) is used as often as the other items in List 2; otherwise students may realise that Item (5) may be disregarded.

(h) The items in List 2 should be arranged in a logical order—for example in ascending order of magnitude (as in Example 8.30), chronologically or alphabetically (for example when listing vitamins).

(i) The stem should, if possible, state the basis for matching. Failure to do so may lead to options which are not homogeneous. Example 8.31 has a poor stem which does not state the basis for matching. A better stem would be 'Match the fish dishes in List 1 with the appropriate accompaniments in List 2.'

EXAMPLES

8.30 *General Engineering/Construction*

Match the S.I. symbols in List 1 with the multiples in List 2.

List 1	List 2
(A) k	(1) 10^{-12}
(B) M	(2) 10^{-6}
(C) p	(3) 10^{-3}
(D) μ	(4) 10^{3}
	(5) 10^{6}

A	B	C	D

8.31 *Cookery/Food Service*

Match the items in List 1 with those in List 2.

List 1	List 2
(A) sole colbert	(1) beurre noisette
(B) sole goujon frit	(2) tomato sauce
(C) plaice à l'Orly	(3) beurre maître d'hôtel
(D) grilled herring	(4) tartare sauce
	(5) mustard sauce

A	B	C	D

Converting Matching Questions to Multiple-choice

(a) A simple way in which part of the information in a matching question may be tested in multiple-choice form is to select one of the items in the list and ask a question around that. Example 8.32 concerns the work on intelligence of four psychologists. Example 8.33 selects one description of such work and asks which of the four was responsible for it. The question could be asked the other way round—for example 'The work on intelligence with which Spearman is associated is . . .'. The resulting multiple-choice questions are easier than the corresponding matching questions, but have the advantage that they are more comparable with usual multiple-choice questions.

EXAMPLES

8.32 *Psychology for Nurses*

Match the names of the psychologists in List 1 with the work on intelligence with which they are associated (List 2).

List 1
(A) Binet
(B) Spearman
(C) Eysenck
(D) Hebb

List 2
(1) arguing that heredity is a major determinant of intelligence
(2) testing children on a large number of items to establish those appropriate to their age
(3) dividing intelligence into Intelligence A and Intelligence B
(4) dividing test questions according to whether they measure general (g) or specific (s) ability
(5) developing performance test of intelligence

A	B	C	D

8.33 *Psychology for Nurses*

The psychologist who divided intelligence test questions according to whether they measured general (g) or specific (s) ability was:

(a) Binet

(b) Spearman

(c) Eysenck

(d) Hebb.

EXAMPLES

8.34 *Food Service*

Match the accompaniments in List 1 with the correct soups from List 2.

List 1
(A) croûtons
(B) rondels of French bread
(C) small patties of duck paste
(D) cheese straws

List 1
(1) bortsch polonaise
(2) tortue claire
(3) purée St. Germain
(4) consommé Madrilène
(5) French onion soup

A	B	C	D

8.35 *Food Service*

From the options below select the one in which the accompaniments in List 1 are correctly matched with the soups in List 2.

(Lists as in Example 8.34.)

	(A)	(B)	(C)	(D)
(a)	3	2	4	5
(b)	3	5	1	2
(c)	4	3	2	1
(d)	5	3	2	4

8.36 *Construction Engineering*

Which identification of the window sections shown is correct?

(1) sill
(2) jamb
(3) transom
(4) mullion
(5) stile
(6) muntin

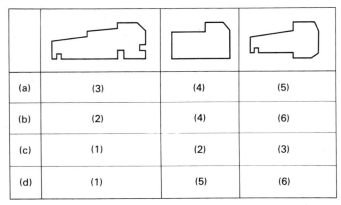

(a)	(3)	(4)	(5)
(b)	(2)	(4)	(6)
(c)	(1)	(2)	(3)
(d)	(1)	(5)	(6)

(b) An alternative method of conversion is to provide four possible ways of matching as the four options and ask the student to select the correct one. Example 8.35 shows how this could be done for the matching question shown in Example 8.34. The multiple-choice question is again easier than the matching question, as the possible choices are limited to four (or five). Since the number of possible combinations greatly exceeds the number of available options, it may be preferable to reduce the number of items to be matched, as has been done in Example 8.36.

Care is needed in choosing the combinations for the options, as the inclusion of an obvious pairing may reveal the key to a student with only partial knowledge. In Example 8.37 the student who knows that (C) is the diameter will choose option (a), even if he does not know any of the other pairings. Example 8.38 is preferable. It might be even better to exclude diameter and radius altogether and concentrate on the possible combinations of arc, chord and tangent.

EXAMPLE

8.37 *Basic Engineering*

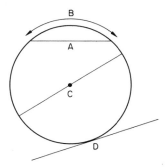

Which of the options below shows correctly the names of the parts of the circle?

(1) radius
(2) diameter
(3) arc
(4) chord
(5) tangent

	A	B	C	D
(a)	4	3	2	5
(b)	1	2	5	4
(c)	5	1	3	2
(d)	2	4	1	3

Example 8.38 is also preferable in that writing out the options instead of using numbers removes an unnecessary stumbling block. This presentation is to be preferred wherever the items in List 2 are fairly short.

Writing 'Order of Events' Questions

'Order of events' questions can be regarded as a special form of matching question, since a given list has to be put into the correct order. The sequence

---

EXAMPLES

8.38   *Basic Engineering*

Which of the following options shows correctly the names of the parts of the circle shown in Example 8.37?

	A	B	C	D
(a)	diameter	tangent	radius	chord
(b)	radius	chord	diameter	tangent
(c)	chord	arc	diameter	tangent
(d)	tangent	arc	diameter	chord

8.39   *Forestry*

Which of the following represents the stages in the life cycle of the large pine weevil (Hylobius abietis)?

(a)   adult — egg — adult

(b)   adult — egg — larva — adult

(c)   adult — egg — nymphal stages — adult

(d)   adult — egg — larva — pupa — adult.

8.40   *Carpentry and Joinery*

The operations involved in constructing a timber floor are listed below. In the boxes provided write the letters of the operations to show the order in which they should be carried out.

(A)   level and fix end joists and trimming joists

(B)   bed wall plates level and true

(C)   set out and cut trimming joists

(D)   level and fix intermediate joists

(E)   cut and fix strutting.

1	2	3	4

may be one observed in nature or science, as in Example 8.39. More often the sequence is that in which a series of tasks should be done, as in Examples 8.40 to 8.43, or the order of priorities (for example, for the nurse in charge of a ward).

Various forms of presentation are possible. Example 8.40 has the form of a matching question with a match panel provided. The other examples are in multiple-choice form. In Example 8.41 the tests listed are numbered and the options consist of possible sequences expressed in numbers. In Examples 8.39, 8.42 and 8.43, the options are written out in full, which is generally easier for the students. An extra complication is added in Examples 8.42 and 8.43, where the items in the list are not the same in each option.

EXAMPLES

8.41 *Electrical Installation*

The tests which should be performed on completion of an installation are:
(1)   test of ring circuit continuity
(2)   tests of effectiveness of earthing
(3)   verification of polarity
(4)   insulation resistance tests.

In which order should they be carried out?
(a)   1, 2, 3, 4
(b)   4, 3, 2, 1
(c)   3, 4, 1, 2
(d)   3, 2, 4, 1

8.42 *General Catering*

In what order should the removal of dust from a variety of surfaces in a room be carried out?
(a)   high dusting, low dusting, vacuum
(b)   low dusting, vacuum, high dusting
(c)   high dusting, sweep, low dusting
(d)   high dusting, vacuum, low dusting.

8.43 *Brickwork*

The joints on the face of a brick building have weathered badly and need repointing. The correct sequence for this work would be to rake out joints and:
(a)   dampen wall, repoint, brush joints starting at the bottom and working up
(b)   repoint, dampen wall, brush joints starting at the top and working down
(c)   brush joints, dampen wall, repoint joints starting at the top and working down
(d)   brush joints, dampen wall, repoint joints starting at the bottom and working up.

A much simpler question is to ask, as in Example 8.44, which of the stated tasks should be done first.

An order of events question may be designed to assess not technical knowledge, but the ability to present material in a logical manner, as in Example 8.45.

Questions of a similar kind may be asked to test knowledge of order of magnitude, as in Example 8.46.

EXAMPLES

8.44 *Soft Furnishing*

After curtains and linings have been cut out, which ONE of the following stages in the making-up process would be completed first?
(a)   stitching the bottom hems on curtains
(b)   lock-stitching linings to curtains
(c)   stitching side seams on curtains
(d)   mitreing corners.

8.45 *Communication Skills*

The following sentences tell the story of a fire at a college, but they are in the wrong order.
(1)   When the alarm was sounded everyone rushed out of the building.
(2)   Eventually the science block was closed down for repairs.
(3)   It was a busy Friday morning at Grafton college.
(4)   The corridors were crowded with students.
(5)   Fire engines soon arrived.
(6)   Some of them saw smoke coming from under the door of the Science Lab.

The correct order should be:
(a)   3   6   1   4   2   5
(b)   3   4   6   1   5   2
(c)   4   6   3   5   1   2
(d)   1   3   6   4   2   5

8.46 *Science Laboratory Technicians*

In which of the following sequences are the compounds arranged in order of increasing molecular weight?
(a)   sucrose, glucose, starch
(b)   glucose, starch, sucrose
(c)   sucrose, starch, glucose
(d)   glucose, sucrose, starch.

Converting True/False Questions to Multiple-choice

Simple true/false questions are not recommended for use, but two or more related true/false questions may form the basis of a multiple-choice question.

The true/false questions may be grouped into a combination question as shown in Example 8.47. Students are asked to say which of the statements are true. This example is not fully satisfactory, as the statements are not closely related, making the question rather a ragbag. Example 8.48 is only a little better in this respect and has the added disadvantage that the number of possible combinations far exceeds the number of options available. Four statements are probably too many for a question of this type.

Example 8.49 is also a combination question, although this is less immediately obvious. It is preferable to the previous two examples because the options are more homogeneous and cover all the possible combinations of

---

EXAMPLES

8.47 *Cookery*

Which of the following statements are true?

(1) Knowledge of the spawning periods of fish is important when purchasing, as the quality of the fish is affected at that time.

(2) For freshwater fish spawning time is usually a close season.

(3) Salt water fish are not protected by a legal close season.

(a) 1 only

(b) 1 and 2 only

(c) 2 and 3 only

(d) 1, 2 and 3.

8.48 *Carpentry and Joinery*

Which of the following statements are correct?

(1) Steel screws should not be used for fixing brass hinges.

(2) Corrugated fasteners are used to join corrugated sheets together.

(3) Oval brads are used for fixing of finishings.

(4) Blued tacks should be used for fixing bituminous roofing felt.

(a) 1 and 3 only

(b) 1 and 4 only

(c) 2 and 4 only

(d) 1, 2 and 3.

valve position. This question might have been derived from a true/false question such as 'During the compression stroke of a four-stroke engine the inlet valve is open. TRUE/FALSE'.

Combination questions are discussed in the next chapter also (see page 127).

APPLICATION

1. For a test with which you are concerned write one or two questions in each of the following categories:

    (a) multiple-response;

    (b) multiple-response converted to multiple-choice form;

    (c) assertion/reason;

    (d) matching;

    (e) matching converted to multiple-choice form;

    (f) 'order of events';

    (g) multiple-choice questions each consisting of a combination of two true/false questions.

    Ask a colleague to comment on your questions.

2. Which of these question types (if any) enable you to test information or abilities not readily capable of being tested by ordinary multiple-choice questions?

EXAMPLE

8.49 *Agricultural Machinery*

During the compression stroke of a four-stroke engine the position of the valves is:

(a) both valves open

(b) both valves closed

(c) exhaust valve open, inlet valve closed

(d) inlet valve open, exhaust valve closed.

9

More Advanced Multiple-choice Question Writing

Chapter 7 outlined the basic rules of multiple-choice question writing and Chapter 8 considered rules for writing other types of objective question and for converting them to multiple-choice format. In this chapter we look at some more advanced techniques for writing multiple-choice questions. The aim of the chapter is to help the writer who has already had some practice in question writing to cover a wider range of topics and abilities, to set more searching questions and to find new ways of testing the same or similar abilities. The section headings are:

setting comprehension and application questions;
testing English;
testing calculations;
setting graphical questions;
setting questions with diagrams;
setting question groups;
finding enough distractors;
setting second and subsequent exams or tests; and
using permutation sets.

When following these guidelines, the writer must, of course, also observe the basic rules give in Chapter 7—the stem must give a clear statement of the problem, the key must be unarguably correct and the distractors unarguably inferior, the right topics and abilities must be tested and irrelevant ones excluded, and so on.

Setting Comprehension and Application Questions

Most writers find it more difficult to set comprehension and application questions than simple factual recall. However, the specification is likely to require them to attempt to test the higher abilities, and comprehension and application questions are often more worth while and more searching than recall. The student who understands and can apply his knowledge is more likely to retain and to use it than the student who simply learns by rote.

A number of different types of problem may be included in the *comprehension* category. Some questions involve the understanding of terms or the ability to translate information from one medium of presentation to another. Example

EXAMPLES

9.1   *Electrical and Electronic Craft*

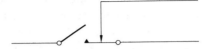

The relay contact set shown above in the released condition is:

(a)   break before make

(b)   make before break

(c)   delayed action

(d)   fast operating.

9.2   *Science Laboratory Technicians*

Which ONE of the following curves of temperature against time shows the way in which a hot solid cools in the laboratory?

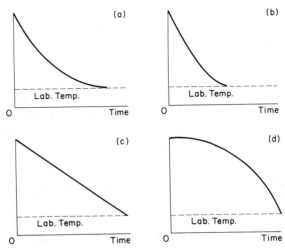

9.1 requires an understanding of the simple diagram shown—a much more complex diagram might be used in another question. Example 9.2 involves the ability to recognise a graphical representation of a common phenomenon. In Example 9.3 the student is required to put into figures what is expressed verbally in the stem. Example 9.4 asks for the meaning of the term, but in this instance, not what the letters R/D stand for, but what they mean in practice.

Many comprehension questions are concerned with the reasons for things; sometimes the reasons for observed facts, as in Example 9.5, and sometimes the reasons which underlie correct practice, as in Example 9.6. Others relate

EXAMPLES

9.3 *Science Laboratory Technicians*

Aluminium has a valency of 3 and oxygen has a valency of 2. What is the formula for aluminium oxide?

(a) Al_3O_2
(b) Al_2O_3
(c) $2AlO_3$
(d) $(AlO_2)_3$.

9.4 *General Catering*

An R/D cheque usually means that:

(a) there is no account in the name of the drawer
(b) there are insufficient funds in the drawer's account
(c) the drawer of the cheque is deceased
(d) there are insufficient funds in the payee's account.

9.5 *Agriculture*

Most farm crops cannot thrive in a waterlogged soil because the soil contains insufficient:

(a) humus
(b) air
(c) plant foods
(d) bacteria.

9.6 *Hairdressing*

The reason for using distilled water to dilute hydrogen peroxide is that it:

(a) has smaller molecules to penetrate the hair
(b) is free from dissolved salts
(c) is slightly alkaline
(d) is slightly acid.

to advantages (as Example 9.7) or disadvantages. Although many such questions include cue words such as 'because', 'reason', 'purpose' or 'advantage', which show that they are intended to test comprehension, others (like Example 9.8) test understanding without the use of such words.

Recall questions may suggest topics for comprehension questions. The recall question shown as Example 9.9 is used as the basis for the comprehension question, Example 9.10, which asks the reason for the correct practice. The two questions would not, of course, appear in the same test. Further questions might be set asking the reason why scion rooting is undesirable or asking students to choose which of four diagrams illustrates correct practice.

EXAMPLES

9.7 *Machine Woodworking*

The cutting action of a rotary shaper cutter block is usually back cutting. The advantage of this is that it:
(a) simplifies the jig design
(b) gives more station positions
(c) needs fewer automatic air cramps
(d) gives a clean and smooth finish.

9.8 *Construction Technicians*

Syphonage is likely to occur in pipe systems when:
(a) pipes of varying diameter are used
(b) too many pipes are joined together
(c) pressure in the pipe is less than atmospheric pressure
(d) the angle of a branch pipe is more than 30° to the vertical.

9.9 *Horticulture*

Grafted fruit trees should be planted so that the position of the union is:
(a) well below soil level
(b) just below soil level
(c) just above soil level
(d) well above soil level.

9.10 *Horticulture*

Grafted fruit trees should be planted with the union well above soil level to:
(a) allow easier cultivation
(b) prevent scion rooting
(c) encourage earlier cropping
(d) assist root action.

Similarly, Example 9.11 is a recall question relating to the requirements of the IEE Regulations concerning the bending of cables. Example 9.12 is a comprehension question which tests partly the same information but partly also whether the student understands what the internal bending radius is. Example 9.13 is another comprehension question, this time asking the reasons for having such a regulation.

EXAMPLES

9.11 *Electrical Installation*

The minimum permitted internal bending radius for a non-armoured, p.v.c.-insulated cable with circular copper condutors and overall diameter less than 10 mm is:

(a) 2.5 times the overall diameter of the cable
(b) 3   times the overall diameter of the cable
(c) 4   times the overall diameter of the cable
(d) 6   times the overall diameter of the cable.

9.12 *Electrical Installation*

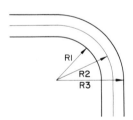

The diagram above shows a bend in a non-armoured, p.v.c.-insulated cable with circular copper conductors of overall diameter 8 mm. The requirements of the IEE Regulations concerning this bend are that:

(a) *R*1 must be at least 2.5 times 8 mm
(b) *R*1 must be at least 3 times 8 mm
(c) *R*2 must be at least 2.5 times 8 mm
(d) *R*3 must be at least 3 times 8 mm.

9.13 *Electrical Installation*

Why do the IEE Regulations lay down a minimum bending radius for cables?

(a) to make installation easier
(b) to encourage economy of materials
(c) to prevent mechanical damage to the conductors
(d) to reduce voltage drop.

The essential feature of an *application* question such as Example 9.14 is that it should require the student to *use* his knowledge or understanding. The problem described must be one with which the student is not already familiar; otherwise the answer becomes a matter of recall not application. Frequently, answering an application question is a two-stage process. For instance, in Example 9.15 the student must first remember the colour coding for resistors, including the significance of the gold band for the tolerance of the rating; he must then calculate the lower limit of possible resistance for the resistor described. In Example 9.16, the student must first decide the criteria for choice (the temperature at which each process has to be carried out) and then decide which of the processes requires the highest temperature.

EXAMPLES

9.14   *Audio-visual Technicians*

In red light, an image of a distant object is focused at 200 mm from an uncorrected lens. Approximately how far from the lens will the image be in blue light?

(a)   190 mm
(b)   200 mm
(c)   210 mm
(d)   220 mm.

9.15   *Electrical and Electronic Craft*

What is the lower limit of resistance of a carbon resistor marked with the following coloured bands — yellow, violet, brown, gold?

(a)   423 Ω
(b)   446.5 Ω
(c)   466.5 Ω
(d)   470 Ω

9.16   *Sheet and Thin Plate Craft*

Which ONE of the following processes would have to be carried out first if they were all to be used on the same small component?

(a)   aluminium riveting
(b)   soft soldering
(c)   fusion welding of copper
(d)   silver soldering.

Some application questions involve a diagram or a rather longer description of the situation to which the student is expected to apply his or her knowledge. In Example 9.17 the student needs to apply his knowledge of the meanings of the symbols used on the diagrams and of the working of this type of circuit. In Example 9.18 he needs to apply his understanding of circuits and his knowledge of the expected values of insulation resistance.

An application question does not always involve a two-stage thought process. Example 9.19 does not obviously do so, but would be classed as application unless the students had been taught this method of correction.

EXAMPLES

9.17 *Radio, Television and Electronics Mechanics*

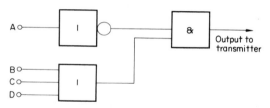

Which ONE of the following inputs to the circuit shown will produce an output?

	A	B	C	D
(a)	1	1	0	0
(b)	1	1	1	0
(c)	1	1	1	1
(d)	0	1	0	0

9.18 *Audio-visual Technicians*

A metal-clad piece of equipment was checked for insulation resistance and the following results were obtained for the resistance between the leads L, N and E.

Resistance	Leads	Equipment switch
4 MΩ	L, N	OFF
3 MΩ	L, E	OFF
200 Ω	L, E	ON

From these results it could be concluded that:
- (a) the apparatus is safe for use
- (b) the apparatus will not function
- (c) the supply current will cause overheating
- (d) there is an earth-leakage fault.

Recall and comprehension questions can often provide a basis or an idea for an application question. Application questions should be as practical as possible, so it is helpful to ask oneself how the student would, in practice, make use of the information he has been taught. If he would not need to use it in practice, then one may wonder why it is being taught at all. Example 9.20 relates to the same information as was tested in Example 9.11, but this time the student is asked to remember the relevant figure and then to apply it to the practical situation described. Example 9.21 tests recall of the ingredients of an hors d'oeuvres dish. Example 9.22 asks the student not only to

---

EXAMPLES

9.19 *Plumbing*

If a vent pipe in a domestic hot water supply system discharges water after the hot taps are used, an accepted manner of correction would be to:

(a)   fit a non-return valve
(b)   reduce the vent pipe diameter
(c)   reduce the cold feed pipe diameter
(d)   heighten the vent pipe.

9.20 *Electrical Installation*

The overall diameter of a non-armoured, p.v.c.-insulated cable with circular copper conductor is 9 mm. The minimum permitted internal bending radius is:

(a)   3 mm
(b)   22.5 mm
(c)   27 mm
(d)   36 mm.

9.21 *Cookery*

The main components of the filling for tomato monégasque are:

(a)   smoked haddock and hard-boiled egg
(b)   poached mussels bound with mustard sauce
(c)   tunny fish and hard-boiled egg
(d)   poached lobster bound with thermidor sauce.

9.22 *Cookery*

Among which ONE of the following hors d'oeuvres variés would a rice salad with prawns best be placed?

(a)   egg mayonnaise, meat salad, tomato monégasque
(b)   potato salad, haricot bean salad, rollmops
(c)   soused herring, pilaff créole, smoked salmon
(d)   potato salad, waldorf salad, cream cheese.

remember the main ingredients of several such dishes, but also to use this information to choose the combination of dishes which would give a suitably varied selection. Example 9.23 asks the student to recall the main ingredients of chicken sauté chasseur. Example 9.24 requires him or her to remember several such items of information and to use them to choose a balanced, varied menu; he should not, for instance, follow mushroom soup with chicken sauté chasseur which also contains mushrooms.

Testing English

Multiple-choice questions cannot, of course, test the student's ability to write an essay or to express himself in prose. They can, however, be used to test a number of aspects of his understanding and use of English.

(a) Reading comprehension can be tested by a question such as Example 9.25.

(b) Identification of unsupported statements and of the basis for making statements can be tested, as in Examples 9.26 and 9.27.

(c) Questions may test spelling or (as in Example 9.28) vocabulary.

(d) Grammar and syntax may be tested, as in Examples 9.29 and 9.30.

(e) Questions may test knowledge of conventions, as in Example 9.31.

All these aspects of the knowledge and use of English may be tested, either on their own or as part of a broader assessment which includes actual prose writing.

EXAMPLES

9.23 *Cookery*

The sauce for chicken sauté chasseur contains:
(a)   sherry and cream
(b)   pimento, mushrooms and sherry
(c)   stock, lemon juice and cream
(d)   mushrooms, tomatoes and white wine.

9.24 *Cookery*

Which ONE of the following options would present the best balanced menu?
(a)   cauliflower soup, sole vin blanc, blanquette de veau
(b)   oxtail soup, sole bonne femme, veal escalope napolitaine
(c)   mushroom soup, sole boistelle, chicken sauté chasseur
(d)   tomato soup, sole dugléré, chicken sauté chasseur.

EXAMPLES

9.25–9.27 *Communication Skills*

From January to December last year 66 local people were killed in road accidents and 954 others were injured. 35 of the fatalities were motor-cyclists or their pillion passengers and 23 were pedestrians. The remaining fatalities were drivers or passengers of other motor vehicles.

A police spokesman stated that the unusually high proportion of fatal accidents might be explained by poor road conditions caused by last year's unusually severe weather. Local motoring organizations agreed with this view.

Questions 9.25–9.27 refer to this passage.

9.25   According to the passage over half the people killed in road accidents last year were:
   (a)   driving in bad weather
   (b)   pedestrians
   (c)   riding motor cycles
   (d)   driving cars or lorries.

9.26   Which of the following statements is NOT supported by the information given in the passage?
   (a)   More pedestrians were killed than motorists.
   (b)   Motor cycles are unpopular with the police.
   (c)   More fatal accidents occurred than was normal.
   (d)   Motoring organizations blamed the bad weather.

9.27   According to the passage, the likelihood that bad weather and road conditions caused the increase in fatal accidents was:
   ,   (a)   the individual opinion of one policeman
   (b)   not supported by statistics
   (c)   the best explanation available
   (d)   not believed by motoring organizations.

9.28   *English for Office Skills*

Which ONE of the following words is closest in meaning to 'synopsis'?
(a)   chapter
(b)   quotation
(c)   extract
(d)   summary.

9.29   *Communication Skills*

Which ONE of the following sentences is correctly written?
(a)   Safety is there responsibility.
(b)   I received a business letter.
(c)   The invoice was not in it's usual place.
(d)   I would of signed it myself.

Testing Calculations

Calculations questions set in objective (or other) examinations have one or both of two broad aims: (a) to test the student's ability to handle numbers and/or formulae and (b) to test his understanding of the relationships between quantities as part of his understanding of the technology of his subject. Calculations which have both aims require the student to understand the underlying technology and also to perform a relevant calculation. The aim of the question affects the way in which it is set. If it seeks mainly to test the student's technical understanding, it may not be necessary to require him to perform the calculation in full—see, for instance, Example 9.32.

EXAMPLES

9.30 *English for Overseas Candidates*

Which of the following options should be inserted in the sentence, 'After searching for hours, . . . we found her.'?

(a)   at last
(b)   lately
(c)   final
(d)   at finish.

9.31 *Communication Skills*

A business letter commencing with 'Dear Sir' should be concluded:

(a)   Yours
(b)   Yours faithfully
(c)   Faithfully
(d)   Truly.

9.32 *Audio-visual Technicians*

v = velocity of sound
f = frequency of a note
λ = the wavelength of this note.

The relationship between them is given by the formula

(a) $f = \lambda v$
(b) $\lambda = fv$
(c) $v = f/\lambda$
(d) $v = \lambda f$.

Wherever possible calculations should be practical in nature and relate to the subject matter of the course. The figures used should be realistic if possible. However, there is no merit in setting calculations with awkward figures, particularly as the time available for a multiple-choice question is only about one minute, and only one mark is available for a correct answer.

The following approaches to setting calculation questions may be used:

(a) The student may be asked simply to identify the correct formula. The terms may be defined, as in Example 9.32, or (if they are well-established conventions) the student may be expected to know them. In Example 9.32 all the options are permutations of the same three quantities. This has the disadvantage that (c) is only a transposition of (a) and the brighter student may appreciate this and discount both options, even if he does not actually know the answer. In other questions the distractors may include quantities not used in the key. For example, a question asking the formula for the area of a circle may have $\dfrac{\pi D^2}{4}$ as the key but use R in the distractors. A question requiring recognition of the correct formula is a recall question.

(b) Students may be asked to transpose a formula, either one which is given, as in Example 9.33, or one which they may be expected to remember. These involve comprehension.

(c) Students may be asked to identify the correct expression, as in Example 9.34. This should be classed as a comprehension question as students will probably not have learnt by heart a formula or expression for this. Hence, they need understanding rather than simple memory to answer the question.

EXAMPLE

9.33 *Motor Vehicle Craft*

Transpose the expression $A = \dfrac{b \times h}{2}$ to make h the subject.

(a) $h = \dfrac{b \times A}{2}$

(b) $h = \dfrac{b}{2 \times A}$

(c) $h = 2 \times b \times A$

(d) $h = \dfrac{2 \times A}{b}$.

(d) Examples 9.35 and 9.36 both require the student to state in general terms the effect of increasing one of the factors in a formula. In Example 9.35 the formula is given; in 9.36 it must be remembered. In both, the emphasis is on the understanding of relationships rather than the ability to calculate out in full.

EXAMPLES

9.34 *Construction Technicians*

The cost of laying a concrete bed in a trench is influenced by the length of the trench, the time taken to lay one metre and the rate of pay per hour. Which of the following expressions shows how to calculate the actual laying cost?

(a) length × time per metre × rate

(b) length × (time per metre + rate)

(c) $\dfrac{\text{length} \times \text{rate}}{\text{time per metre}}$

(d) $\dfrac{\text{length} \times \text{time per metre}}{\text{rate}}$.

9.35 *Electrical Installation*

A circular conductor of diameter D mm has a cross-sectional area of:

$$\frac{\pi D^2}{4} \text{ mm}^2$$

If the diameter is doubled, the cross-sectional area will be:

(a) doubled

(b) four times greater

(c) π times greater

(d) π^2 times greater.

9.36 *Motor Vehicle Craft*

If the diameter of a cylinder liner is doubled whilst its length remains constant, the external surface area will be:

(a) doubled

(b) trebled

(c) multiplied by four

(d) squared.

(*e*) In Example 9.37 the student is required to substitute the correct values in a formula. This should be classed as application rather than comprehension, since the student must recall the correct formula as well as make the necessary substitution. Requiring him to carry out the calculation as well would have little value in relation to the extra time needed.

(*f*) Example 9.38 requires the student to carry out a fairly straightforward calculation and arrive at the answer. This should, however, be classed as application since the student must decide the method for himself.

EXAMPLES

9.37 *Sheet Metal and Thin Plate Craft*

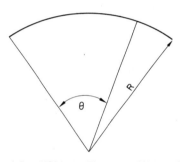

In the diagram $\theta = 80°$ and $R = 420$ mm. The area of the template is equal to:

(a) $\dfrac{\pi \times 420 \times 80^2}{360}$ mm^2

(b) $\dfrac{\pi \times 420^2 \times 80}{360}$ mm^2

(c) $\dfrac{2 \pi \times 420 \times 80}{360}$ mm^2

(d) $\dfrac{\pi \times 420^2 \times 360}{80}$ mm^2.

9.38 *Carpentry and Joinery*

What measurement of boarding would be required to cover an area of floor joists 3 m by 2 m using a board of covering width 125 mm? (Ignore any waste allowance and assume joists span shortest direction.)

(a) 16 metre run

(b) 26 metre run

(c) 48 metre run

(d) 98 metre run.

(g) Questions may give students the appropriate formula and values and ask them to carry out the calculation with that data. Such questions test comprehension rather than application. However, in Example 9.39, the student must see the need to transpose the formula as well as insert the appropriate values and then calculate, so this question may be classed as application.

(h) A question such as Example 9.40, which leaves the student to choose the appropriate formula and then use it in the problem given, is testing application.

(i) A diagram may be needed in order to pose the problem clearly, as in Examples 9.37 and 9.41.

The figures used as distractors in multiple-choice calculation questions should not be just plucked out of thin air, but should be chosen on a logical basis and reflect likely errors of method or computation. Distractors may be based on:

(a) use of the wrong formula, as in option (c) of Example 9.37 and options (b) and (d) of Example 9.40

(b) a muddled use of the correct formula, as in options (a) and (d) of 9.37, or incorrect transposition, as in (a) and (b) of Example 9.39.

EXAMPLES

9.39 *Motor Vehicle Craft*

The area of a triangle is given by

$$A = \frac{B \times H}{2}.$$

If $A = 360\,\text{mm}^2$ and $H = 24\,\text{mm}$, the value of B is:

(a) 7.5 mm
(b) 15 mm
(c) 30 mm
(d) 45 mm.

9.40 *Electrical Installation*

Three cables have insulation resistances of 20 MΩ, 5 MΩ, and 4 MΩ respectively. If the three are connected in series, the combined insulation resistance will be:

(a) 2 MΩ
(b) 9.66 MΩ
(c) 20 MΩ
(d) 29 MΩ.

EXAMPLES

9.41 *Sheet Metal and Thin Plate Craft*

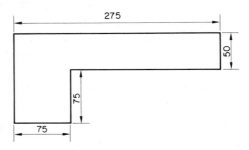

Which ONE of the following gives a minimum size of sheet required for SIX of the blanks shown in the diagram?

(a)   350 mm × 125 mm
(b)   350 mm × 250 mm
(c)   350 mm × 375 mm
(d)   350 mm × 750 mm.

9.42 *Cookery*

Sixteen portions of roast chicken can be cooked in a microaire oven in 12 minutes, as opposed to a conventional oven cooking 32 portions in one hour. Over a two-hour period the difference in output would be:

(a)   16 portions   [32 − 16]
(b)   32 portions   [(32 × 2) − (16 × 2)]
(c)   48 portions   [(16 × 5) − 32]
(d)   96 portions   [(16 × 5 × 2) − (32 × 2)]

9.43 *Electrical Installation*

If a 10 Ω resistor is dissipating 1000 W the current flowing is:

(a)   0.1 A
(b)   1 A
(c)   10 A
(d)   100 A.

9.44 *Construction Technicians*

A 100 mm length of steel rod of cross-sectional area 100 mm^2 extends by 1 mm under a load of 200 kN. What is the value of the strain in the rod?

(a)   0.02 kN/mm^2
(b)   0.01 kN/mm^2
(c)   0.01 MN/mm^2
(d)   0.01.

(c) likely errors of calculation, as in Example 9.42. (The figures in brackets have been added to show the method by which each option was obtained; they would not appear in the actual examination.)

(d) misplacing of the decimal point, as in Example 9.43.

(e) mistakes over units, as in Example 9.44.

Setting Graphical Questions

Multiple-choice questions may be set to test understanding or use of graphs and also of histograms, phasor diagrams, pie charts and similar methods of presenting information. Several different aims are possible for questions of this type, and it is important to be clear what the aim of the question is since it will influence the way the question is set. Possible aims are:

(a) to test the student's ability to read and derive information from a graph, bar chart or similar diagram, as in Examples 9.45 to 9.47. These questions require fairly accurate answers, so careful drawing to scale is necessary.

These questions do not require the students to use any technical knowledge of the subject matter of their course—they are concerned solely with their understanding of graphical methods of presentation.

A simple graph may not offer enough possible plausible distractors to provide the basis of a question. If the graph given in Example 2.2 (p. 11) had only one curve, it would be impossible to make a question with any likely distractors from it. A more complex graph must therefore be provided.

(b) to test understanding of information presented graphically, as in Example 9.48. Although this question is mainly concerned with the interpretation of the graph, it also requires an understanding of the relevant technology, and so differs from Examples 9.45 to 9.47. However, like them, it requires accurate drawing of the graph.

The examples of graphical questions given so far test comprehension.

(c) to test ability to use a given graph in solving a problem, as in Example 9.49. Here the actual reading of the graph is a relatively minor part of the question. The student must also know how to use the information to solve the given problem. This question tests the student's ability to apply his knowledge.

EXAMPLES

9.45—9.47 *Communication Skills*

Questions 9.45—9.47 refer to the bar chart which shows the tonnage of shipping launched in various countries between 1950 and 1975.

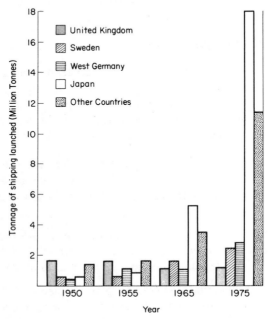

9.45 According to the bar chart the country which shows the greatest increase in launchings since 1950 is:

(a) Japan

(b) other countries

(c) West Germany

(d) Sweden.

9.46 The country which has shown a decrease in launchings is:

(a) Sweden

(b) West Germany

(c) United Kingdom

(d) Japan.

9.47 The launchings from Japanese shipyards since 1950 have increased by approximately:

(a) 175 000 tonnes

(b) 1 000 000 tonnes

(c) 4 350 000 tonnes

(d) 17 500 000 tonnes.

EXAMPLES

9.48 *Radio, Television and Electronics Mechanics*

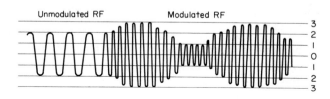

Unmodulated RF   Modulated RF

What is the depth of modulation of a.m. wave shown?

(a)   33 ⅓ %

(b)   50%

(c)   66 ⅔ %

(d)   100%.

9.49 *Photography*

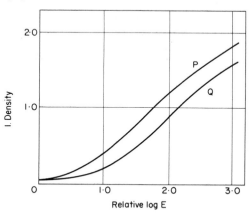

The figure shows the characteristic curves of two films processed under certain development conditions. The correct exposure, for a particular subject, is 1/30 s at f/8 for material P. Using the same exposure time, which ONE of the following will be the correct aperture for material Q?

(a)   *f*/4

(b)   *f*/5.6

(c)   *f*/11

(d)   *f*/16.

This type of question also requires accurate drawing of the graph and the provision of grid lines to help the student read it correctly.

(*d*) to test the student's knowledge and understanding of the general shape of particular characteristic curves. The graphs may be very simple indeed, as in Example 9.50, or more accurate, as in Example 9.51. However, it is not necessary for the graphs to be drawn very precisely—only the general shape is required.

Questions of this sort are designed to test the student's technical understanding, rather than his ability to use graphs, and the graphs are merely the medium for presentation of the question. Questions of this type usually test comprehension.

EXAMPLE

9.50   *Radio, Television and Electronics Mechanics*

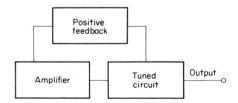

The output from the circuit shown will be:

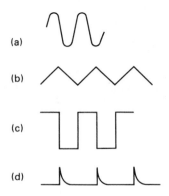

Frequently these questions require the provision of four separate graphs from which the student must choose the correct one. Sometimes, as in Example 9.51, it may be possible to draw the four curves on the same axes. This both saves on space and printing costs, and makes it possible for the same diagram to be used with a slightly different question in a future paper.

Setting Questions with Diagrams

As with graphical questions, questions including diagrams may have a number of different aims. In some the diagram is merely an aid to an understanding of the question; in others the question aims to test under-standing of diagrams as such. In any case it is important that the diagrams should be clearly drawn and should conform to the appropriate British Standards. Whether or not the diagram needs to be drawn accurately to scale depends upon the requirements of the question; usually a fully accurate, scaled drawing is not needed in multiple-choice questions.

EXAMPLE

9.51   *Electrical Craft*

Typical performance curves for current, power factor, efficiency and slip of an induction motor are shown below. Which curve shows the efficiency of the motor?

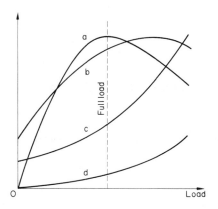

The aims of a question using a diagram may include:

(*a*) using the diagram to make the question clearer. This is so in Example 9.52, which would be difficult to express using words only. In many subjects diagrams are a natural means of expression and should therefore be used freely in questions.

(*b*) testing the student's recognition of an object depicted, as in Examples 9.53 and 9.54. These are factual recall questions and test the student's technical knowledge—the diagram is simply a medium of expression for the question.

EXAMPLES

9.52 *Sheet Metal Craft*

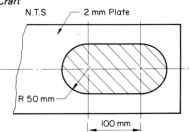

The shaded area of metal shown is most accurately removed by:

(a)   blanking with circular and square tools

(b)   a trepanning tool

(c)   bandsawing

(d)   oxy-fuel gas cutting.

9.53 *Footwear Manufacture Operatives*

Which one of the following basic styles is shown by the shoe above?

(a)   Ghillie

(b)   Gibson

(c)   Monk

(d)   Chelsea.

(c) testing the student's knowledge of drawing symbols and conventions, as in Example 9.55. This is also a factual recall question.

(d) testing the student's understanding of the purpose or working of the object or circuit depicted, as in Example 9.56. Questions based on circuit diagrams would also come into this category (see Examples 9.65—9.69).

EXAMPLES

9.54 *Heating and Ventilating Fitting*

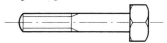

The component shown is a:
(a)   coach bolt
(b)   stud
(c)   bolt
(d)   set screw.

9.55 *Machine Woodworking*

The diagram shows the British Standard 1192 symbol for:
(a)   hardboard
(b)   insulation board
(c)   plywood
(d)   fibreboard.

9.56 *Machine Woodworking*

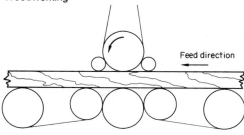

Billy Roll Feed

The type of feed arrangement shown is used for:
(a)   feeding short stock on a four-sided moulder
(b)   transfer of materials on double end tenoners in tandem
(c)   accurate thicknessing of thin material on wide belt sanders
(d)   applying adhesives to flat panels for veneering.

In these questions the emphasis is once again on the technical knowledge of the students, with the drawing used simply as part of the means of communication.

Questions may test both technical knowledge and knowledge of drawing conventions, and many drawing questions at higher levels are likely to do both. However, the examples given above show that diagrams are perhaps more likely to be used to aid understanding of the question than as an aim in themselves.

Most of the examples given so far in this section use a single diagram as part of the stem, but questions may also require students to choose from four diagrams provided. Such questions may be used to test knowledge of drawing conventions, recognition of objects, working methods, etc., as in Example 9.57, or understanding of the technology, as in Examples 9.58 and 9.59. Questions using four diagrams require more work in both setting and printing and are consequently more expensive to produce. Sometimes, if there is a need to reduce costs, it may be possible to turn the question round and use only one diagram. For instance, the diagram of option (d) of Example 9.57 might be printed as part of the stem and students asked to state which of four types of bond was represented. Example 9.59 might be revised as shown in Example 9.60, but this is less easy to follow than the original. Example 9.58 could not reasonably be asked without the use of four diagrams. The general

EXAMPLE

9.57 *Roadwork*

Which one of the following sketches represents court bond?

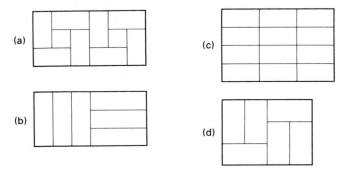

EXAMPLE

9.58 *Mechanical Engineering Craft*

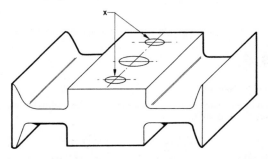

The light alloy component shown above is to be clamped before the holes X are drilled. Which of the clamping arrangements shown below will support the component fully during drilling?

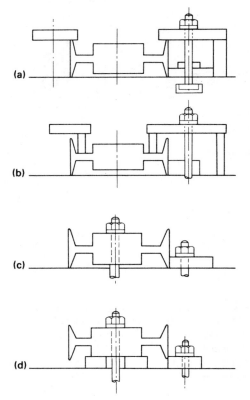

preference should be to use whichever method of presentation is clearest for the student. If two methods are equally clear, then the less expensive will, of course, be preferred.

EXAMPLES

9.59 *Electrical Installation*

The ohmic value of a resistor is to be measured using the voltmeter and ammeter method. The correct circuit is shown in:

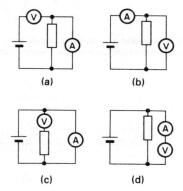

9.60 *Electrical Installation*

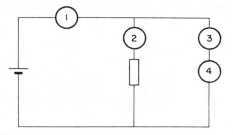

The value of the resistor in the circuit shown is to be measured using the voltmeter and ammeter method. The correct positions of the instruments would be:

(a) voltmeter at 1, ammeter at 4
(b) voltmeter at 4, ammeter at 1
(c) voltmeter at 2, ammeter at 3
(d) voltmeter at 4, ammeter at 3.

Setting Question Groups

A 'question group' consists of a number of questions all related to a central problem and usually based on some introductory material. Sometimes, as in Examples 9.25—9.27, the introductory material consists of a passage of prose.

EXAMPLES

9.61—9.64 *Mechanical Engineering Craft*

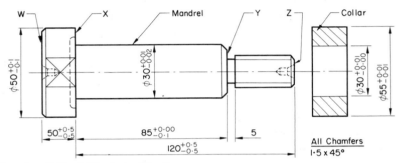

Questions 9.61—9.64 refer to this diagram.

9.61   The main datum for length measurements in the diagram above is:
  (a)   W
  (b)   X
  (c)   Y
  (d)   Z.

9.62   To give maximum metal conditions the collar diameters must measure:
  (a)   30.01 and 55.01
  (b)   30.00 and 54.99
  (c)   30.01 and 54.99
  (d)   30.00 and 55.01.

9.63   Quantities of the mandrel shown in the diagram are to be turned in lathe. A suitable gauge for checking $85^{+0.00}_{-0.1}$ dimension during manufacture would be:
  (a)   go and no-go caliper gauge
  (b)   vernier caliper gauge
  (c)   go and no-go depth gauge
  (d)   vernier height gauge.

9.64   The bore of the collar is to be a clearance fit on the mandrel. This means that the HIGH LIMIT of the mandrel must be:
  (a)   less than the low limit of the bore
  (b)   less than the high limit of the bore
  (c)   greater than the low limit of the bore
  (d)   greater than the high limit of the bore.

More often, as in Examples 9.61—9.64, the introductory material consists mainly of a diagram. In medicine and nursing, similar question groups may be set around a case history and the 'case history' approach has also been tried for management and industrial relations subjects.

Question groups have a number of advantages.

(a) The questions can be made more relevant and practical if they are based on a realistic diagram or problem.

(b) It may be easier to set application questions by this method.

(c) Questions related to several different syllabus topics may be set on one problem, thus emphasising the inter-relationship between syllabus sections.

(d) The student is able to concentrate on the various aspects of a single problem, rather than having to switch his attention from one topic to another in a series of unrelated questions.

(e) It is possible to use larger, more complex diagrams and longer case descriptions, which it would be unreasonable to expect the student to master just for one question.

(f) Setting a number of questions on one diagram makes more economical use of the diagram.

(g) The student is required to select that part of the information in the diagram or passage which is relevant to each question.

The following points should be observed when setting question groups:

(a) The introductory material, i.e. the diagram or passage, should be realistic, posing a practical problem or situation. It should not be excessively long or complex, but must be capable of forming the basis of a number of questions, preferably relating to several syllabus topics.

(b) The number and quality of the questions set should be worthy of the introductory material—they should offer a reasonable reward for the time the student has spent reading and comprehending the material.

(c) The questions used in any one examination or test should not overlap or give the answer to one another. However, extra questions may be set for use in subsequent tests.

(d) The paper or test as a whole must conform to the specification, so that in any one test the number of questions in the group which relate to one syllabus topic and ability must not exceed the number given in the specification. However, extra questions on the same topics and abilities may be saved for future use.

EXAMPLES

9.65—9.69 *Electrical and Electronic Craft*

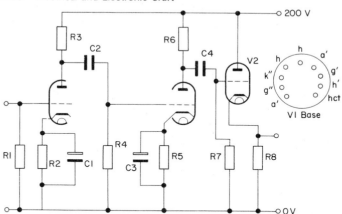

Examples 9.65—9.69 refer to this diagram.

9.65 In the circuit shown the gain of each of the first two stages is 20. The overall amplifier gain is:

(a) 20

(b) 40

(c) 200

(d) 400.

9.66 In the circuit shown the reduction in gain at low frequencies is due to:

(a) increased reactance of C2 and C4

(b) reduced reactance of C2 and C4

(c) increased reactance of C1 and C3

(d) reduced reactance of C1 and C3.

9.67 In the circuit shown the phase angle between input and output at normal operating frequency is:

(a) 0°

(b) +90°

(c) −90°

(d) 180°.

9.68 In the circuit shown the type of capacitor normally used for C4:

(a) has an air dielectric

(b) has a mica dielectric

(c) has a waxed paper dielectric

(d) is electrolytic.

9.69 In the circuit shown a suitable value for R4 is:

(a) 100 Ω   (c) 100 kΩ

(b) 1 kΩ   (d) 10 MΩ.

(e) If possible the questions in the group should relate to a number of different syllabus sections. This is the case in Examples 9.65—9.69 where the questions test mainly understanding of the circuit, but also knowledge of types of capacitor and calculations on amplification.

(f) The answer to one question in the group should not depend upon the student's having answered a previous question correctly—each question should be capable of being answered on its own.

(g) It is permissible to include in the group one or two questions which could be 'free-standing', i.e. which could appear without the diagram and without the rest of the group. Example 9.65 is such a question—slightly rephrased it could be used without the diagram. However, a question group should not consist entirely of such potentially free-standing questions.

(h) All the questions in the group should appear on one page or on facing pages.

(i) The introductory material should state clearly which questions constitute the group. If possible there should be an indication of the end of the group, so that the student knows that the next question is unrelated.

Finding Enough Distractors

Finding sufficient good distractors is a problem for the more advanced question writer just as for the novice. A four-option question with one weak distractor is effectively a three-option question and therefore more guessable for the student who does not really know the answer.

The following suggestions may help in finding enough suitable distractors:

(a) Set the question to some students as a short-answer question and see what answers are given. This is an old tip, still worth trying, though it may not be possible with all types of question or in a single-college examination. However, there is no point in using as a distractor the silly answers given by the weakest class member—they are not likely to be plausible to anyone but him or her.

(b) Define the class of the options. If the stem is well written, the distractors will all fall into a particular category. In Example 9.70 all the options are definitions of terms used on bottles of German wine. These are likely to be more plausible distractors than terms which the writer invents.

(c) Think round the problem and look for distractors in related subject matter. Example 9.71 asks for an advantage of using projects, option (a) being the key. Option (b) is an advantage of examinations, not shared by projects; options (c) and (d) are advantages of objective or structured questions but not of projects. It would not, of course, be a plausible distractor to state 'it is difficult to be sure that the work is the student's own'; this is often true of projects, but is clearly a disadvantage, so will not be chosen, even by the student who is unsure of its truth. A similar thought process has been used in writing the distractors for Example 9.72; each of the distractors is something which is achieved by some other method of treating milk (evaporating, homogenising, sterilising).

(d) Turn the question round by writing a stem based on the key. Sometimes a question which lacks plausible distractors in one form may be workable if turned round. For instance, a question which asked 'What term is used to describe food prepared in accordance with Jewish dietary laws?' might lack suitable options to go with 'kosher', but the question may be reversed to ask for the meaning of the term 'kosher', as in Example 9.73

EXAMPLES

9.70 *Food Service*

The term 'auslese' on a bottle of wine means that the grapes used to make the wine are:
(a) late gathered
(b) gathered after a frost
(c) selected individual grapes from selected bunches
(d) from selected bunches.

9.71 *Achievement Testing*

One advantage of using a project to assess student performance is that:
(a) it can test the ability to collect and organise relevant information
(b) it is easy to be sure that the work is the student's own
(c) the answers of all students follow a similar pattern, making marking easier
(d) broad and consistent syllabus coverage can be achieved.

9.72 *Cookery*

The pasteurisation of milk is carried out in order to:
(a) evaporate water content
(b) destroy pathogenic bacteria
(c) distribute cream evenly
(d) destroy heat-resistant spores.

(*e*) Rewrite the question to test a different ability. Ways of rewriting recall questions to test comprehension and application were discussed on pages 98—103.

EXAMPLES

9.73 *Food Service*

The term 'kosher' is used of food which is prepared:
(a) especially for Jewish feasts
(b) in accordance with Jewish dietary regulations
(c) in accordance with Hindu dietary laws
(d) for Muslims to eat at the end of Ramadan.

9.74 *Electrical Craft*

If the voltage applied to a circuit is increased, the current in the circuit will:
(a) increase
(b) decrease
(c) remain the same
(d) ?

9.75 *Carpentry and Joinery*

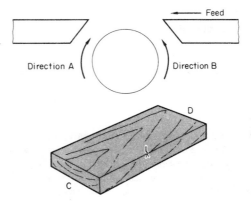

A cutterblock in a hand surfacing machine is shown in the diagram together with a length of timber with the direction of the grain indicated. The face and edge marks denote the surfaces to be planed. Which one of the following gives the best finish to the face of the timber?
(a) cutter direction A, timber planed D end first
(b) cutter direction B, timber planed D end first
(c) cutter direction A, timber planed C end first
(d) cutter direction B, timber planed C end first.

(*f*) Accept that some questions simply do not have four possible options. Questions concerning the effect on (a) of an increase in (b), like Example 9.74, pose a particular problem. There just is no possible fourth option and option (c), 'remain the same', is unlikely to be plausible. This particular example should probably be discarded, but in some cases it may be possible to use such a question as a basis for further work. Example 9.75 shows how a pair of two-option questions (on cutter direction and which end to plane first) may be combined to make a viable four-option question. Another example was given in Chapter 8 to show how a multiple-choice question might be derived from a true/false question (see Example 8.49, page 94).

In Example 9.75 each option consists of two factors. In some questions it is possible to limit each option to one factor by bringing in a reference to apparently related statements which are in fact irrelevant to the question. This has been done in Example 9.76. This question has basically only two options ((a) and (d)), but by bringing in the irrelevant question of which metal conducts heat more rapidly, the writer has contrived to make two more options ((b) and (c)). This is only possible if the new distractors appear relevant to the less knowledgeable student.

(*g*) Make each option a combination of factors. The use of combination questions was considered in Chapter 8 as a means of converting multiple-response questions to multiple-choice. The examples considered then involved combinations of two or three from up to six factors. However, combination questions can also be used where there are only three or four factors, and can be used to solve the problem of the fourth distractor.

EXAMPLE

9.76 *Plumbing*

A bi-metal thermostat composed of a brass tube and an invar steel rod works because:
(a)   invar steel expands more than brass
(b)   invar steel conducts heat rapidly
(c)   brass conducts heat rapidly
(d)   brass expands more than invar steel.

Example 9.77 shows how such a question may be set using combinations of two from four factors. However, it is not necessary to have four factors; as shown in Example 9.78 a viable question may be written using combinations of only three factors.

Questions of this type should be used sparingly. They are more difficult for students to answer than the simple multiple-choice type and require mental agility which may not be relevant to the subject being tested. They are not always the most suitable method of dealing with the problem of insufficient distractors.

Combination questions must be set with care to ensure that there are no clues to give the answer away. The factors in the list must all be plausible; if one is obviously wrong, then any options in which it is included will be immediately seen to be wrong. Even if the factors are all plausible, the student may be able to deduce the answer from partial knowledge; in Example 9.78 the student who knows that (1) is wrong can

EXAMPLES

9.77 *Roadwork*

A Cowley level can be used on site to set out:
(1)   the alignment of a horizontal curve
(2)   the profile of a vertical curve
(3)   gradients and transfer levels
(4)   the line of a radius curve.

Which ones are correct?
(a)   1 and 2
(b)   1 and 4
(c)   2 and 3
(d)   3 and 4.

9.78 *Roadwork*

A Cowley level can be used on site to set out:
(1)   the alignment of a horizontal curve
(2)   the profile of a vertical curve
(3)   gradients and transfer levels.

Which ones are correct?
(a)   2 only
(b)   1 and 3 only
(c)   2 and 3 only
(d)   1, 2 and 3.

eliminate options (b) and (d); if he also knows that (3) is correct, he can select (c) as the answer without knowing anything about factor (2). However, if they are carefully set, combination questions can be a useful way of assessing student knowledge in areas which are difficult to test.

Setting Second and Subsequent Examinations or Tests

The question writers who have struggled to produce enough good questions for one examination may well be daunted by the prospect of having to produce a second examination, and a third, and perhaps a pretest as well. The good questions from the first examination will be banked for reuse, but there will be other questions which prove unsatisfactory in practice and need replacement. In any case one can hardly set substantially the same paper year after year. So where are the new questions to come from?

One priority is, of course, to try to set questions on topics or subdivisions of topics which have not previously been examined. This is essential if the syllabus coverage is to be complete over a period of several examinations. However, it will still be necessary to produce new questions to test knowledge the same as, or very similar to, that which was tested in the first paper set. There are a number of ways in which new questions may be generated from existing ones, some of them producing questions testing the same knowledge and abilities, others testing different facets of the same information, or different abilities.

(*a*) Change the stem so that one of the distractors becomes the key. For instance, Example 9.70 (on page 125) could be changed to ask for the meaning of 'spätlese'; the same four options could be used, but the key would become (a).

(*b*) Ask the opposite question. Example 9.79 asks which of the given four soil

---

EXAMPLE

9.79 *Horticulture*

Which ONE of the following soil types would warm up most quickly in the spring?
(a) sand loam
(b) silt
(c) sand
(d) clay loam.

types warms up most quickly in spring. Using the same four options, a question could be asked on which warms most slowly. Obviously, not all questions lend themselves to this treatment.

EXAMPLES

9.80   *Food Service*

A German wine made from the grapes of selected bunches would be described as:
(a)   spätlese
(b)   beerenauslese
(c)   auslese
(d)   eiswein.

9.81   *Radio, Television and Electronics Mechanics*

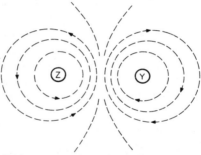

To produce a magnetic field pattern as shown in the diagram, the direction of current flow in conductors Z and Y must be:

(c) Reverse the stem and the options. This has already been suggested as a method of finding enough distractors; if there are enough distractors already, it may be used as a method of generating another question. Example 9.70 which asked for the meaning of 'auslese' could be turned round as shown in Example 9.80. This method may also be used for questions which include diagrams. Example 9.81 may be turned round as shown in Example 9.82.

Reversing the question is not always possible, either because there are insufficient options or because the question is not practical or realistic if reversed.

EXAMPLE

9.82   *Radio, Television and Electronics Mechanics*

Which of the following diagrams shows correctly the magnetic field pattern round the two conductors?

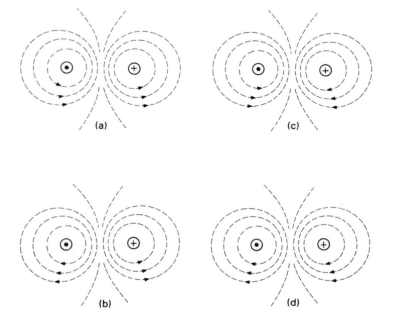

(d) Vary the closeness of the distractors. This affects the difficulty of the question, so must be done with caution. Example 9.83 can be answered correctly by the student who knows that poppadums are associated with Indian cookery. Example 9.84 is more difficult, requiring a more precise knowledge of what a poppadum is. Two of the distractors are also accompaniments to Indian meals.

EXAMPLES

9.83 *Food Service*

A poppadum is a:
(a)   name given to a selection of Chinese dishes
(b)   type of French vegetable dish
(c)   variety of Italian pizza
(d)   thin fried pancake served with Indian dishes.

9.84 *Food Service*

A poppadum is a:
(a)   cocktail savoury on a stick
(b)   strip of dried fish
(c)   dried, highly seasoned lentil pancake
(d)   thick round piece of unleavened bread.

9.85 *Electrical Installation*

The maximum permitted space factor for cables installed in conduit is:
(a)   35%
(b)   40%
(c)   45%
(d)   55%.

9.86 *Electrical Installation*

The space factor of 40% for cables installed in conduits may be slightly exceeded if:
(a)   the conduit is short and straight
(b)   there are not more than two 90° bends
(c)   the inner radius of the bends is at least 2.5 times the cable diameter
(d)   the ambient temperature is below 20 °C.

9.87 *Electrical Installation*

The requirements of the IEE Regulations concerning space factor in conduits are that:
(a)   at least 35% of the space must be left free of cables
(b)   not more than 35% of the space may be occupied by cables
(c)   at least 40% of the space must be left free of cables
(d)   not more than 40% of the space may be occupied by cables.

(e) Progress from recall to questions testing comprehension and application. This was illustrated on pages 98—103.

(f) Ask questions on different applications of the same knowledge. If this is simply a matter of varying the figures used in calculation it is likely to be easy. If it requires the invention of a quite different situation in which the student must apply his knowledge, it will probably be more difficult to write.

Some of these methods of generating new questions from an existing one are illustrated in Examples 9.85—9.89. Example 9.85 is a simple factual recall questions. Example 9.86, which also tests recall, asks for the permitted exception to the rule. Example 9.87 tests both whether the student can remember the correct figure and also whether he appreciates what the figure refers to; it therefore tests comprehension. Example 9.88 tests the application of the same knowledge to a particular conduit. The distractors in Example 9.88 are designed to attract the student who forgets to multiply the factor (a), the student who misremembers the figure to use (b) and the student who thinks that the 40% refers to the space not the cable (d). Example 9.89 is obtained by reversing the original question (Example 9.85).

The IEE Regulations also specify space factors for ducts and trunking, so a similar set of questions could be set on these also. Probably not more than one or two such questions should appear in any one paper, but from the one original question (Example 9.85) the writer now has material covering this topic for a number of examinations.

EXAMPLES

9.88 *Electrical Installation*

The internal cross-sectional area of a conduit is $200 \, mm^2$. The maximum total cross-sectional area of the cables which may be drawn into it is:

(a) $40 \, mm^2$
(b) $60 \, mm^2$
(c) $80 \, mm^2$
(d) $120 \, mm^2$

9.89 *Electrical Installation*

The IEE Regulations specify a space factor of 40% for cables run in:

(a)   short straight ducts
(b)   ducts with not more than two bends
(c)   conduit
(d)   trunking.

Using Permutation Sets

As the discussion earlier in this chapter has shown, there are many instances where a number of different questions may be asked to test one item of knowledge. It is sometimes helpful to write down all the possible keys and distractors in the form of a 'permutation set'. Example 9.90 shows the base material of a number of such permutation sets, testing fairly basic knowledge of vitamins such as might be expected in a domestic cookery or catering course.

EXAMPLE

9.90   *Nutrition*

Vitamin	Soluble in	Necessary for	Deficiency diseases	Found in	Examples of foods
A	Fat	Growth Vision Resistance to infection	Stunted growth Susceptibility to infection Night blindness	Animal fats Developed from the carotene in green vegetables, yellow fruit and carrots	Milk, butter, cheese, cabbage, carrots
B_1	Water	Metabolism Nutrition of nerve cells	Beriberi	Husks and germ of cereals and pulses	
B_2	Water	Functioning of cell enzymes			
B_{12}	Water	Development of red cells in bone marrow	Pernicious anaemia	(To a lesser extent) in vegetables, fruit, milk, eggs, meat	Wholemeal bread, brown rice, yeast
C	Water	Resistance to infection Wound repair	Scurvy	Fresh fruit (particularly citrus) Green vegetables Potatoes	Oranges, lemons, cabbage, sprouts, potatoes
D	Fat	Development of bones and teeth Utilisation of calcium and phosphorus	Rickets	Animal fats Cod and halibut liver oil	Milk, butter, cheese, cod liver oil
E	Fat	Uncertain		Vegetable oils Cereals	
K	Fat	Blood clotting	Tendency to haemorrhage	Green vegetables Liver	Cabbage, sprouts, Liver

Examples 9.91—9.93 show the types of question which may be set on this base material. For each stem one or two possible keys are shown and a number of distractors. For an actual examination or pretest the writer would select one key and three distractors.

The advantage of writing out the questions in this way is that the maximum number of potential questions is identified with the minimum of effort. A large stock of possible questions is available for use in future examinations. If a team of two or three writers has worked on the production of the permutation set, they know that there is no point in trying to write further questions

EXAMPLES

9.91 *Nutrition*

Vitamin A is necessary for:

keys	growth
	resistance to infection
	proper vision.
distractors	metabolism
	nutrition of nerve cells
	development of red cells
	development of bones and teeth
	blood clotting:

9.92 *Nutrition*

A deficiency of Vitamin D leads to:

key	rickets
distractors	night blindness
	beriberi
	pernicious anaemia
	scurvy
	tendency to haemorrhage.

9.93 *Nutrition*

Which of the following is the best source of Vitamin B complex?

keys	wholemeal flour
	yeast
distractors	milk
	cheese
	eggs
	green vegetables
	citrus fruits.

to test the same knowledge and abilities, so the likelihood of unintended overlap between the questions set by different writers is reduced.

The base material of Example 9.90 can give rise to many more questions than have been shown. Each of Examples 9.91—9.93 may be asked concerning other vitamins, and their converse may also be asked; for example the converse of Example 9.91 would be 'The vitamin necessary for proper vision is . . .'. Not all possible variations are viable, however. For instance, it would not be possible to write a simple multiple-choice question asking of which vitamin green vegetables are a good source; there are too many keys and not enough distractors. A combination question (see page 127 above) might be feasible.

Some possible questions are likely to be considerably easier than others, even with the same stem. In Example 9.91 'proper vision' is likely to be better known than 'growth' or 'resistance to infection'. In Example 9.92 'night blindness', 'beriberi' and 'scurvy' may be less plausible distractors than the other two. Consequently it is still desirable to pretest the exact question wherever practicable.

Writers still learning the craft of question writing and those preparing their first examination will probably not find the idea of the permutation set very helpful. They should concentrate on producing the required number of acceptable questions. Permutation sets are more useful to an established team of writers seeking to set new questions on topics which have already been tested several times, particularly if a number of examinations are required each year.

However, writers should not fall into the trap of trying to set whole examinations by means of questions extracted from permutation sets. That would make the examinations stereotyped. Fresh questions are needed in each examination or pretest, particularly in the application category.

APPLICATION

1. Select one or two recall questions from a test you have set, or one with which you are concerned. Use them as a basis for setting:

    (a) comprehension questions (ask 'Why is it so?', 'What are the advantages?', etc.);

    (b) application questions (ask yourself how the student will use this information in his work, then set a question requiring him to use the information in that way).

2. Write questions of different styles, as suggested in this chapter, to test each of the following:

    (a) understanding and use of English;

    (b) calculations;

    (c) graphs;

    (d) understanding and use of diagrams.

3. Select a suitable diagram, prose passage or case history, and write a 'question group' based on it.

4. Use the suggestions in the section 'Finding Enough Distractors' to rewrite questions which have previously caused you problems.

5. Select an existing question and write as many (good) variations on it as possible.

6. Prepare the base material for a 'permutation set' and draft a few questions based on it.

Ask a colleague to edit your questions.

10

Editing and Paper Compilation

In this chapter we look at the procedures needed for editing questions, compiling pretests and papers from unpretested questions and checking the compilation. 'Editing' is the process by which draft questions are checked for suitability and clarity by a small panel of subject and testing experts. For a paper which is to consist of unpretested questions, the usual order of events is:

questions written;

questions edited by panel;

satisfactory questions compiled into a paper;

compilation checked by at least one other person.

Sometimes, in an attempt to shorten the process, the editing panel is presented with a complete paper of draft questions to edit. This is usually less satisfactory. There may be too much work to complete in one session and the editors may feel inhibited from rejecting weak questions because they know that replacements must be found immediately.

When a pretest is being prepared the stages are the same as shown above, except that it is not essential for the compilation of the pretest to be checked by a second person.

Why Edit?

Draft questions are edited to try to ensure the validity and reliability of the paper. To ensure *validity* the panel should check that the questions are all within the syllabus and specification, are relevant to the occupations of the students and are of approximately the right level of difficulty. This is necessary because teachers may disagree on the interpretation of the syllabus; even colleagues within a single college may have somewhat different interpretations and if the examination is shared between several colleges the differences will probably be greater.

To ensure *reliability* the editing panel should check that the questions are clearly written, technically accurate and have a single correct answer (or, for multiple-response, the stated number of keys). This is necessary because what seems to the writer to be perfectly clear may be far from clear to the students. Also, the answer which the writer considers correct may be a matter of opinion or local usage, not supported by colleagues or students with a slightly different background. Options intended as distractors may be justifiable answers in some situations.

Who Should Edit?

All questions should be edited by at least two people other than the writer; editors should be subject experts, with knowledge of the subject content, the course and the students. There should be at least one editor who is fully conversant with the techniques of objective testing; this may be one of the two subject experts, but could be a third, 'lay' editor. It is sometimes useful to have an editor who is not an expert in the subject being assessed; he or she can identify clues, implausible distractors, and questions which test only general intelligence, which the subject experts may well miss. If the non-subject-expert can answer the question, then there is very possibly something wrong with it! The question writer should also normally be present at the editing meeting. He should be willing to listen and respond to reasoned criticism, and the editors should be courteous and constructive in their comments.

If the questions have been written by a team of people, then less formal editing is needed. It is usually sufficient for a single person, outside the team, to vet the questions.

The Conduct of the Editing Meeting

The following suggestions are intended to ensure that the meeting of the editing panel is as effective as possible and makes the best use of the time of the people attending it.

(*a*) Copies of the questions should be circulated to the editors about a week before the meeting is to be held.

(*b*) Editors should do their homework by reading through the questions in advance, so that they come to the meeting with their comments prepared.

(*c*) The key to each question should not be marked on the question itself. The editor should decide for himself which is intended to be the answer, and may then check (perhaps from a separate list at the end) that his view agrees with that of the writer. If writer and editor are not agreed on the answer, how can the student be expected to know it? The editor's decision should not be influenced by seeing what the writer considers to be the key. For this reason, the keys to the examples given in this book are listed separately at the end.

(d) The syllabus reference and the ability tested should be marked against the question and the editor should check that they are correct. A question can be perfectly acceptable in itself, but allocated to the wrong section or ability.

(e) The meeting of the panel need not be conducted too formally, but it is helpful for someone to act as chairman, to pace the meeting and to ensure that time is not wasted, that everything is given adequate consideration and that a decision is reached concerning each question.

(f) Someone should act as secretary, to keep a record of the modifications made and of any questions rejected or referred back to the writer for change. If necessary, the secretary should read out the modified version of the question to ensure that it is what each of the editors think they are agreeing—in a confused discussion, where several different modifications are proposed, it is easy for two members to have different impressions of what was actually agreed.

Checklist for Editing Individual Questions

The desirable characteristics of an objective question were discussed at some length in Chapter 7 and the underlying reasons, in terms of validity and reliability, in Chapter 3. It is therefore not necessary to repeat here the reasons *why* the following questions should be asked of each draft objective question.

(a) Is the question within the syllabus and specification?

(b) Are the syllabus reference and ability tested correctly stated?

(c) Is the question appropriate and relevant? Is it something which the student *should* be able to answer? (It is possible for a question to be technically within the syllabus and still be silly or irrelevant.)

(d) Does it test appropriate abilities and exclude, as far as possible, irrelevant ones (such as reading skill or mental agility if these are not essential)?

(e) Is the question of the correct level (not too easy or too difficult) and of the correct length?

(*f*) Is all necessary information provided?

(*g*) Is the question clearly presented in the stem? (Can the bright student anticipate what the answer will be before he reads the options?)

(*h*) Is the question as concise and unambiguous as possible?

(*i*) Is the question presented in the best possible manner? Would a diagram make it clearer? Would an alternative question type (e.g. multiple-response or matching) be clearer?

(*j*) Do the editors agree that the key is unarguably correct (or that all keys are correct in a multiple-response question)?

(*k*) Are all the distractors unarguably wrong or (in a 'Which is the best' question) inferior to the key?

(*l*) Are all the distractors plausible to the level of student being assessed?

(*m*) Is the question free of clues which may guide the less knowledgeable student to the answer?

(*n*) Are the options given in a logical order?

(*o*) Are the grammar, spelling, terminology, abbreviations and units correct?

Compiling a Pretest or Examination Paper from Unpretested Questions

When all the questions have been edited and sufficient satisfactory questions approved, it is necessary to compile from them a pretest or examination paper, as required. The points listed below should be observed. It should be noted that the questions will already have been edited and approved, so that the suitability of individual questions is not at issue; the concern now is to put them together to form an acceptable test.

(*a*) An examination paper *must* conform to the specification. A pretest should normally follow the specification fairly closely, but some variation is permissible, either because insufficient questions are available for a particular topic, or because it is necessary to pretest extra questions in one area to fill a gap in the bank.

(*b*) The test should contain some easy and some hard questions—it may be difficult to gauge the degree of difficulty with certainty. The test should begin with some easy questions.

(*c*) In all pretests and examinations of a particular paper there should be a reasonably consistent percentage of any special question types used, for example questions with diagrams, questions involving calculations and non-multiple-choice objective questions.

(d) There should be no discernible pattern in the distribution of the keys; there should not, for example, be a long run of (a)s or (b)s or a repeat of (a), (b), (c), (d), (a), (b), (c), (d). In the test as a whole the proportion of each letter should be about the same. It is not necessary to go to great lengths to achieve a random distribution of keys. If several writers have been involved and each has distributed the keys equally between the options, then the end result is likely to be a reasonably random distribution.

(e) If it does prove necessary to change the position of the keys in some questions, care must be taken not to disrupt a logical sequence of options or an ascending order of numerical options.

(f) The questions selected for the test must not overlap in content. There is a particular danger of this if two similar questions have been classed under different syllabus headings.

(g) One question should not give away the answer to another, or give a strong clue.

(h) Each question should be independent; the answer to one question should not depend upon the student having answered a previous question correctly.

Checking the Compilation

If it is an actual examination which has been compiled, a second person should check that all the points listed above have been observed. He or she should also check that any list of keys which has been prepared is correct.

For a pretest, a check on the compilation is not essential.

APPLICATION

1. What editing procedures are used for the objective tests with which you are concerned? Are they adequate?

2. Using the checklist given in this chapter, edit the questions in a test you have used recently, or some questions you have set. What modifications to the questions would you recommend?

3. Check the compilation of a test or pretest with which you are concerned. Does it conform to the recommendations of this chapter?

11

Test Instructions and Layout

Even when enough good questions have been written and edited and a test compiled, the task of test production is not over. The test still needs a heading and instructions (sometimes referred to together as the 'rubric') and still needs to be printed or duplicated. These may seem relatively minor jobs, but it is still important that they are done accurately. However good the questions, the test will be a poor one if the instructions are unclear or the typing full of errors—or even if the students arrive to take the test at the wrong time!

Test Heading

The precise content of the test heading will depend on whether it is a pretest or an examination, whether it is a national or a college test, and so on. However, the following items usually need to be included in the heading:

course title, including level;
question paper title, if the course has more than one paper;
reference number, if applicable;
whether pretest or examination;
date and time;
duration;
requirements for each student (usually only pencil and rubber, but may include mathematical tables, calculators and reference material);
number of questions in the test;
number to be attempted (usually all);
penalties for guessing (if applicable);
instructions on how to answer the questions.

Example 11.1 shows one of the possible ways of presenting this information, excluding the actual instructions for answering, which are discussed in the next paragraph. There are other equally acceptable methods of presentation.

Instructions on Answering

It is essential that the instructions to the students on how to answer the questions are absolutely clear. It is also highly desirable that the students should have some practice in the mechanics of answering objective questions (for example in the use of a separate answer sheet) before they take the test.

The instructions should normally be accompanied by an example of how to record the answer chosen, and should include instruction on what to do if the student changes his mind as to which answer is correct.

The content of the instructions will depend on whether the answers are to be made in the test booklet or on a separate answer sheet, what types of question are used, how the options are lettered (a, 'a', (a), A, (A), etc.) and so on. The examples provided are by no means the only possible ways of giving the instructions.

EXAMPLE

11.1 *Test Heading and Instructions*

Basic Cookery for the Catering Industry	You should have the following for this test:
(Pretest)	this pretest booklet a test answer sheet an HB pencil an India rubber
Test number 706-1-01 F	Time allowed 2 hours

The test which you are about to take consists entirely of multiple-choice questions. The Institute is testing these questions to determine their suitability for use in future examinations and welcomes your assistance. Please treat this test as though it were a real examination and give the best answer you can to each question.

The time allowed for this test is shown above. The time allowance is generous and you will have no need to hurry. Please indicate the time you spent answering the questions in the space provided on your answer sheet.

You will be told the results of the test, but they will not affect your results in any future examination which you might take.

The success of this pretesting depends to a large extent on you and we are most grateful for your help.

Any calculations or rough work can be done in this pretest booklet.

Answer all 100 questions. If you find a question difficult, leave it and return to it later.

Example 11.2 shows instructions for a test which is to be answered on a separate answer sheet to be machine marked. In this instance, the use of the correct type of pencil is essential and this point should be emphasised to students. Example 11.3 shows instructions for multiple-choice questions to be answered on the test booklet itself. This is rather easier for the students, but does not normally allow machine-marking, and makes manual marking more tedious.

EXAMPLES

11.2 *Instructions for Using Separate Answer Sheet*

You MUST use an HB pencil to complete ALL parts of the answer sheet.

Each question shows FOUR possible answers (lettered (a), (b), (c) and (d)); only ONE is correct. Decide which one is correct and fill in the appropriate space on your answer sheet with your HB pencil. For example, if you think (c) is correct, fill in the appropriate space like this:

20.

If you want to change your answer, rub it out thoroughly. Then fill in the box which you have now decided is correct.

11.3 *Instructions for Answering on the Test Booklet*

Each question has FOUR possible answers (lettered (a), (b), (c) and (d)); only ONE is correct. Decide which one is correct and put a ring round the letter beside it. For example, if you think that the answer to this question is (b), draw a ring round (b) like this:

A table top faced with plastics laminate would have a compensator on its lower edge to prevent:

(a)   chipping
(b)   bending
(c)   breakage
(d)   shrinkage.

If you want to change your answer, cross out your first ring and draw a ring round the letter next to the answer you now think is correct, like this:

(a)
(b)
(c)
(d)

Machine marking is usually only possible for multiple-choice questions, so questions of other types are generally answered on the test booklet. If the test includes questions of more than one type, it is best to put the instructions for answering each type at the head of the questions to which the instructions refer. Thus the question paper heading might contain only a brief reference to the types of question included in the test. This would be followed by the instructions for answering multiple-choice questions, the multiple-choice questions themselves, the instructions for answering multiple-response questions, the multiple-response questions themselves, and so on. Examples 11.4–11.6 show instructions for answering question of other types.

Test Layout

The following points concerning the layout of the printed or duplicated test paper should be noted.

(*a*) Questions are easier to read if each of the options begins on a new line, as in the examples in this book.

(*b*) It is sometimes an advantage to arrange the questions in two columns. This allows the use of shorter lines (which are easier to read) without wasting space.

(*c*) The system by which the options are lettered (using a to d, (a) to (d), A to D, etc.) is not important. What is important is that the system should be used consistently throughout the paper and that the letters against the questions should be consistent with those in the instructions and those on any separate answer sheet.

(*d*) A match panel should be provided for answering matching questions, as shown in Example 11.6.

(*e*) A question should not be split between two pages or columns.

(*f*) Diagrams must be on the same page as the questions to which they refer, or at the very least, on the facing page.

(*g*) 'See next page' or similar should be printed at the foot of each right-hand page, where necessary.

(*h*) If the questions are to be answered on the test booklet, there should be enough space for the students to ring the chosen option letter; this may necessitate double spacing of the options.

(*i*) All questions of one type (multiple-choice, multiple-response, etc.) should be grouped together. Multiple-choice, which are the easiest on average, should come first.

EXAMPLES

11.4 *Instructions for Answering Multiple-response Questions*

Each question has SIX possible answers (lettered (a) to (f)); MORE THAN ONE are correct. Decide which ones are correct and draw rings round the letters next to them. For example, if you think that the answers to this question are (a), (d), (e) and (f), draw rings like this:

Which FOUR of the following are ingredients of a zabaglione?

ⓐ   egg yolks
(b)   egg whites
(c)   cream
ⓓ   sugar
ⓔ   white wine
ⓕ   zest of lemon.

If you want to change your answer, cross out the ring which you think is wrong, and draw a ring round the letter beside the answer you now think is correct, like this:

⊗
ⓑ
(c)
ⓓ
ⓔ
ⓕ

11.5 *Instructions for Answering Assertion/Reason Questions*

Each question consists of an Assertion and a Reason. You have to decide whether each of them is a true statement and, if so, whether the Reason is a correct explanation of the Assertion. Decide which of the five possible answers you think is correct and put a ring round the letter beside it. For example, if you think the correct answer to this question is (a), draw a ring round (a) like this:

ASSERTION		REASON
On a large welded segmental bend the joints of the segments are positioned alternately to one-another	BECAUSE	this saves material.

ⓐ   Both assertion and reason are true statements and the reason is a correct explanation of the assertion.
(b)   Both assertion and reason are true statements, but the reason is not a correct explanation of the assertion.
(c)   The assertion is true, but the reason is a false statement.
(d)   The assertion is a false statement, but the reason is true.
(e)   Both assertion and reason are false statements.

If you want to change your answer, cross out the ring and draw a ring round the answer which you now think is correct, like this:

(b)
ⓒ
(d)
(e)

EXAMPLE

11.6   *Instructions for Answering Matching Questions*

Each question consists of two lists, which have to be matched. Use the 'Match panel' to match the items in List 2 to those in List 1. Note that there will be one item in List 2 which is not used. For example, if you think that diagram A shows English bond, B shows stretcher bond and so on, fill in the 'Match panel' like this:

List 1

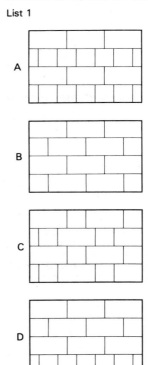

List 2

(1) Flemish bond

(2) English bond

(3) English garden wall bond

(4) Court bond

(5) Stretcher bond.

Match panel			
A	B	C	D
2	5	1	3

If you want to change your answer, cross it through and write below what you now think is the answer, like this:

Match panel			
A	B	C	D
~~2~~	~~4~~	~~1~~	~~5~~
2	4	1	5

(*j*) Within each grouping of questions, the easiest should come first and the most difficult at the end.

(*k*) Questions of medium difficulty are best arranged according to topic. Students find this easier than having to make mental switches from one topic to another and back. Arranging all the questions in strict order of increasing difficulty does not help the student—he is not likely to recognise that Question 59 is 1% easier than Question 60.

(*l*) It is useful to provide a place at the end of the test (or at the end of the answer sheet) for students to indicate how long they took to answer the questions (see Example 11.7). This information can be valuable when the results of the test are reviewed (see Chapter 14).

(*n*) If the questions have been designed for self-testing, for example for revision purposes, it is necessary to provide a separate section at the end showing the answers. These should be overleaf from the last of the questions.

Test Printing or Duplication

The individual college lecturer is likely to have little say in how the test is duplicated or (exceptionally) printed. If there is a choice, some form of lithographic process using paper masters is preferable to old-style stencils, particularly if diagrams are needed. For small numbers, photocopying may be the most economical method. The 'copy' given to the typist or printer must be clear and correct. Particular care is needed with units, abbreviations,

---

EXAMPLE

11.7 *Instructions for Indicating Time Taken*

Please indicate how long you spent answering the questions by ticking the appropriate box.

Less than 1 hour	1 to 1¼ hours	1¼ + to 1½ hours	1½ to 1¾ hours	1¾ to 2 hours	Not finished after 2 hours

symbols, Greek letters and foreign terms, particularly the accents. The typist or printer is not a subject expert and cannot be expected to correct errors in the specialist vocabulary of the subject.

The typing or typesetting must be checked carefully before printing. Consider Example 11.8 and note any errors. This example will be discussed at the end of this paragraph.

In the interests of security it is best not to produce many more copies than are likely to be needed, although it is advisable to have one or two spares.

The 'answer key' which lists the answers to each of the questions in the test must be double-checked against the test as printed; the order of the questions may have been changed slightly to fit the available space. The person responsible should check by reading the questions, not by referring to an earlier list of keys which might contain errors.

Let us now turn back to Example 11.8. Four errors have been introduced into this example:

(1) 'Following' is misspelt.

(2) The question mark at the end of the stem has been omitted.

(3) Option (b) should read 'fish meal'.

(4) Option (d) has been wrongly labelled (c).

The fourth mistake is the most serious and would be even more so if either (c) or (d) were the key. The mistake in (b) may cause some confusion, but again is less serious than if it involved the key. The mistakes in the stem, if they occurred in the printed version of the test, would merely be evidence of sloppy typing and checking. They would not, however, tend to inspire confidence in the reliability of the test.

EXAMPLE

11.8 *Agriculture*

Which ONE of the folowing is classified as a carbohydrate concentrate.
(a)   rolled barley
(b)   fish meat
(c)   meat and bone meal
(c)   cracked beans.

Security

Objective questions are often banked, both to make best use of the effort which has gone into their setting and to enable accurate comparison of standards from year to year (see Chapter 16). Consequently, security is even more important than with ordinary examinations, and continues to be important after the test has been held. All copies of the test paper must therefore be collected at the end of the test. Copies must not be allowed outside the examination room, although it is usual to allow interested lecturers to view the test in the room—but not, of course, to take copies. These rules are slightly easier to enforce if the students answer on the test paper itself.

After the test has been taken, spare copies of the test should be destroyed, only one or two being retained in a secure file. Alternatively, if it is intended to reuse exactly the same test with another group of students, clean copies should be kept under lock and key. Any breach of the security of the test questions threatens the validity and reliability of future tests, which is not in the true, long-term interests of students, staff, employers, or the public.

APPLICATION
Check the heading, instructions and layout of a test with which you are concerned.

1. Does the heading contain all necessary information?

2. Are the instructions clear?

3. Does the layout conform to all the recommendations of this chapter?

4. Are there any errors in the typing or printing?

5. What arrangements are used to ensure the security of the questions? Are they adequate?

PART IV

Marking and Result Determination

12

Marking and Scoring Systems

The aim of this chapter is to examine the available methods of:

(*a*) marking—finding how many questions each student has answered correctly;

(*b*) scoring—allocating marks to each student's answers. (Although the usual rule is one mark per correct answer, variations are sometimes proposed.)

Marking Systems

The individual lecturer is unlikely to be able to decide completely for himself what system of marking (manual or mechanical) to use, simply because not all the possible systems are available to him. However, he may be able to influence the decision of his college or other body as to what hardware, if any, is to be purchased.

In deciding on a system, those responsible should consider, not only what is the easiest way to mark the answers of each student, but also how the answers can be analysed (see Chapter 15 for the analysis of individual questions).

The prices and availability of hardware are likely to change considerably, but in general the marking methods available fall into the following categories:

1. *Manual marking of answers made on the test booklet itself.* Answering on the test booklet is easier for the students and should possibly be preferred for lowest level courses, but it makes marking and analysis more tedious. There are more pages to turn and a greater bulk of paper to handle than if a separate answer sheet is used, and it is more difficult to use templates to aid marking.

When a test booklet is being marked, the number of correct responses on each page (or on each double-spread) should be totalled and an overall total found at the end. A second person should check the marking and totalling on scripts which are near the pass/fail borderline.

2. *Manual marking of a separate answer sheet.* This is easier than marking answers made on the test booklet, as there are fewer pages to turn. A template can be used and can greatly assist marking; one method is to mark the correct answers on a translucent sheet which will fit over the student's answer sheet. It is then necessary only to count the number of times that the student's answer coincides with that on the template. However, it is important to check that the template is correctly aligned over the student's answer sheet, and that the student has not marked more answers to a question than are required. A second person should check the marking of borderline answer sheets. Although the marking is easier, it is still necessary to do the analysis manually which is tedious.

3. *Computer-marking and analysis from punched cards.* In this system, the students' responses (usually made on a separate answer sheet) are punched onto cards or tape and processed through an appropriate computer program, which can give both the marks for each student and the analysis of each question. This is obviously easier for the lecturer, but is much more expensive as it requires specialist staff for punching and operation and access to an appropriate computer program. It is perhaps rather more likely to give errors than manual marking and certainly more error-prone than optical mark-reading.

Computer programs have generally been developed only for multiple-choice questions, but would work also for assertion/reason if designed to cope with five options. Special answer sheets and programming would be required for multiple-response and matching questions.

4. *Marking and analysis by micro-computer.* Recent innovations have made such machines as micro-computers, capable of multiple-choice analysis, available at prices within the reach of a college and possibly even of a college department. Input of students' responses may be via a simple keyboard, making specialist punching staff unnecessary; however, the possibility of mistakes in keying in the responses remains. Input may also be from optically-read bar-codes, with a very low error rate.

Such a system offers considerable advantages over manual marking and analysis, saving lecturer time and increasing the range of analysis available.

5. *Optical marking-only machines.* There is at least one fairly inexpensive machine on the market which can mark multiple-choice answers much more

quickly than a human marker. The error rate from a machine of this type is likely to be much lower than from manual marking, although it is still wise to give an extra check on borderline cases, particularly if there is evidence of the student having changed his mind about the answer and rubbed out. It may also be necessary to check visually that only one answer has been marked to each question. A basic machine of this sort does not give analysis, but it does speed up the job of marking, which is a necessary preliminary to manual analysis.

6. *Optical marking scanner, linked to computer for analysis.* In this system, everything is automatic; the specially printed answer sheets are 'read' by a machine which is linked to a computer programmed to produce both marks for individual students and analysis of questions. The hardware for this system is, of course, very expensive and at present beyond the means of many establishments. Also, since the system is in its infancy, there may be severe 'teething troubles', particularly if students have not followed the instructions carefully. However, for those able to afford it, a fully automatic system offers enormous advantages in speed, saving of lecturer time and range of analysis available. Initially, such a system is likely to be designed to cope only with multiple-choice or assertion/reason questions.

Scoring Systems

The simplest and most usual method of scoring is to award one mark for each multiple-choice question answered correctly. No mark is awarded if the student has marked more than one answer as correct.

One mark is awarded for each assertion/reason question answered correctly.

One mark is awarded for a multiple-response or matching question which has been answered entirely correctly. No mark is given if the answer is partly correct (for example if the student has correctly indicated two of the three keys in a multiple-response question) and no mark is given if the student has marked more than the required number of options.

Other, different, scoring systems have been proposed at times for multiple-choice questions. One of these is to use a differential scoring system, giving, say, two marks for each fully correct answer and one mark for the choice of a distractor which is inferior to the key, but not completely wrong. Some have also suggested deducting one or two marks from students who select an option which is dangerous or unhygienic. A scoring system of this sort is not recommended, however.

(*a*) It greatly complicates the scoring without giving an undisputed benefit.

(*b*) Questions cannot necessarily be written to fall into this mould; it would not be possible to write every question so that it had a distractor worth one mark as well as a key worth two marks and two other distractors. Question writers face enough difficulties as it is.

(*c*) The distinction between 'near miss' distractors, worth one mark, and 'wrong' distractors, worth no marks, is likely to be largely subjective.

(*d*) Dangerous or unhygienic distractors, penalised by deducting two marks, would be plausible only to a small minority of students, and so would detract from the value of the test as a measuring instrument for the majority of students. This device might, however, be useful as a teaching measure, provided it was followed by a classroom discussion which established the reasons why the distractor was so unsatisfactory.

The limitations of using a correction for guessing in multiple-choice papers were discussed in Chapter 5. Such a correction is not needed for multiple-response or matching questions, where the chances of guessing correctly are minimal, and should probably not be used at all in a mixed paper which includes either multiple-response or matching questions.

In general it is best to avoid the use of a guessing correction in entirely multiple-choice papers also. If it is decided to use a correction, the score of each student may be obtained from:

$$S = R - \frac{W}{3}$$ (for four-option multiple-choice questions)

or $$S = R - \frac{W}{4}$$ (for five-option multiple-choice and assertion/reason questions)

where

S is the student's corrected score,

R is the number of questions answered correctly, and

W is the number of questions answered wrongly.

APPLICATION

1. Review the marking arrangements for tests with which you are concerned. Is sufficient care used, particularly in checking borderline scripts?

2. What other marking systems are available to you? Would they offer any increase in accuracy or efficiency?

3. Justify any special scoring systems used.

13

Result Determination

When the marking is complete it is necessary to decide, or perhaps merely to confirm, the pass mark and, if appropriate, the distinction or merit mark. If possible some analysis of the way the paper and the individual questions have performed should be undertaken first (see Chapters 14 and 15). At the very least the mean and standard deviation for the whole test should be calculated (see Chapter 14 and Appendix A).

If the questions are banked and reused, it is relatively easy to maintain a constant standard from year to year, as will be discussed later in the chapter. However, it is necessary to make a judgment as to the standard to be set for the first examination or test and this is not as easy as might be supposed.

Methods of determining results for a single test are traditionally described as being either *criterion-referenced* or *norm-referenced*.

Criterion-referencing

In a criterion-referenced system, the criteria for success are laid down in advance—before the course even begins. The student who fulfils all the stated criteria passes the assessment. This sounds attractive and for certain assessment areas, for example some types of practical skill, it is both the most valid and the most reliable system. If a student is required, as one of the criteria, to file a given material to stated dimensions, within a stated tolerance and a stated time, then it is easy to assess whether he has fulfilled this criterion. For an objective test of cognitive abilities criterion-referencing cannot so easily be applied.

(a) The questions set in any one test cover only a sample of the syllabus. The sample chosen, even though it covers all the major areas of the syllabus, may happen to contain easier or more difficult topics.

(*b*) The difficulty of the questions on any single topic might vary; for example some application questions on a particular topic may be easier than others.

(*c*) Altering the distractors for a question can alter its difficulty. As was shown in Chapter 9 (p. 132, Examples 9.83 and 9.84), two questions with the same stem but different options may have different levels of difficulty.

(*d*) A paper composed of more discriminating questions (i.e. those which distinguish best between the more and less able students) has a higher standard deviation (or spread of marks) and this affects the pass rate, even if the mean is unchanged. This effect is explained later in this chapter (p. 162).

It follows that it is not possible to specify a uniform pass mark of, say, 50 or 60 for an objective paper. The level of attainment represented by a mark of 50 will vary from test to test as the difficulty and discriminating power of the questions vary. Only if the standard of the questions is held constant can the pass mark remain the same from year to year. In any case, stating that the student shall pass if he answers 50% of questions correctly is not an objective criterion if the standard of the questions cannot be specified precisely.

Norm-referencing

In a norm-referenced system, the result of each individual student is determined by his position in relation to the rest of the population for the test or examination. It may, for example, be decided to set the pass mark so that 80% of the student population will pass. If this approach is associated with large-scale pretesting and banking of the questions, so that their standard is maintained from year to year (or so that the same, secure test is used each year), then the level of attainment of the students passing will be constant.

Sometimes, however, norm-referencing is interpreted to mean that the same percentage of students should pass each year, regardless of variations in the ability of the students or the difficulty of the test. Manifestly, this is potentially unjust in a small-entry or single-college examination where the standard of the students may vary from year to year—the bottom student of a generally bright class will fail, but may actually have reached a higher standard than the middle student from a mediocre class who passes the next year. In a large national examination it is likely that the overall standard of the students will remain the same from year to year, and the system may therefore be fair, but without pretesting and banking there is no in-built guarantee that it is.

In any case, the decision of what percentage of students to pass is largely arbitrary.

It follows that there is no simple route to result determination and that neither criterion-referencing nor norm-referencing should be used alone, without question banking.

Before going on to consider how the examiner should in fact decide the pass mark, it is necessary to show how the mean and standard deviation of the marks affect the pass rate.

The Effect of the Mean and the Standard Deviation

The mean and the standard deviation are also discussed (in the context of test review) in Chapter 14 and methods of calculation are demonstrated in Appendix A.

The mean mark for the test is the average mark obtained by the students who took it; the higher the mean for a given test, the better the students; conversely, the higher the test mean obtained by a particular group of students, the easier the test. Other things being equal, a higher mean will give a higher pass rate. This is illustrated in Example 13.1, which shows the

EXAMPLE

13.1   *Effect of Mean and Standard Deviation on Pass Rate*

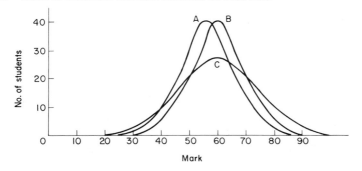

results on three tests, each taken by 1000 students. Test B has a higher mean than Test A, and if the pass mark for each is 45, more students will pass on Test B.

Other things are not always equal, however. The pass rate is also affected by the standard deviation, which is a measure of the spread of marks; the larger the standard deviation, the more widely spread are the students' marks. This is illustrated by Tests B and C in Example 13.1. These two tests have the same mean (60) and the same number of students (1000), but Test C has a larger standard deviation (15, compared with 10 for A and B). In Test C there are fewer students near to the mean and more at the ends of the range. With a pass mark of 45 for each, the percentage of students who pass Test B will be higher than the percentage who pass Test C.

For each of these three tests the distribution of marks is symmetrical and in fact conforms to the 'normal curve' in which there is a known relationship between the distance of a mark from the mean (expressed in number of standard deviations) and the percentage of students at or above that mark. However, for a much smaller number of students, the distribution of test marks may well not be 'normal'. For an objective test the distribution may be not symmetrical but 'negatively skewed', with students concentrated at the top end of the scale and a 'tail' at the bottom end, as shown in Example 13.2.

EXAMPLE

13.2 *Negatively Skewed Distribution*

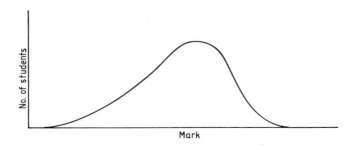

Deciding the Pass Mark for the First Examination

The decision of where to put the pass mark is one which must be taken by a subject expert with knowledge of the technology, the industries concerned, the course and the general abilities of the students on the course, as well as of the test content and the way in which the questions have been answered. The following points should be considered when determining the pass mark:

(a) A high standard does not necessarily require a high failure rate. If the students have been appropriately selected and well taught, and are adequately motivated, few if any need fail.

(b) A higher failure rate than expected may indicate that one or more of the conditions in (a) has not been fulfilled. Alternatively, it may indicate that the test has been pitched at the wrong level.

(c) If the mean and standard deviation are not what the question setters anticipated, this may indicate real shortcomings in the students' attainment. However, it may similarly indicate a fault in the examination itself. It may be difficult for the examiners or lecturers concerned to decide which of these factors apply.

(d) The analysis of individual questions may well shed light on the performance of the test as a whole (see Chapter 15 for review of individual questions). If a large number of the questions have been excessively easy, or difficult, or have not discriminated well, this will affect the value of the test as a measuring instrument. If possible, questions should be analysed before the results are decided, and very poor questions excluded from the result.

(e) There may be other evidence of the students' attainment, for example in other papers taken or in the results of projects or course-work assessment. In general, however, the results of other assessments will be less reliable than those of the objective paper.

Deciding the Pass Mark for Subsequent Examinations

If the examination or test is to be reliable, the standard of attainment required for a pass must be the same in subsequent years as for the first examination. Therefore, unless there are real grounds for believing that the standard has been pitched at the wrong level, the priority in future years will be to keep the pass standard the same. This does not necessarily mean that the pass *mark* should remain unchanged since, as we have seen, the tests will not necessarily all be of the same level of difficulty. It does mean attempting to relate each year's test to earlier ones and to equate the level of attainment represented by the pass mark in this year with that in earlier years; for example a mark of 55 in one year may represent the same absolute level of attainment as a mark of 50 in a previous year, and the pass mark set should take account of this. The following points may help to relate the students and the test of one year to those of a previous year:

(a) In a large national examination it is reasonable to expect that the overall level of students will stay much the same from year to year, and investigation is needed if the level of attainment appears to have changed markedly. Factors which may lead to a real change in the national standards of students in a course include syllabus or course pattern changes, changes in the pattern of employment or the standard of recruitment, changes in the unemployment figures (which may in turn affect the standard of young people being recruited into the industry), changes in secondary education and so on.

(b) In a single-college examination, it is a little less likely that the standard of the students will remain the same from year to year, although it may do so—for example if there is a major local employer with a consistent recruitment policy.

(c) Colleges may have other evidence as to the general standard of the students in a particular year, for example their performance on a standardised entry test. In general, evidence from course-work is likely to be less reliable than the objective test.

(d) By far the best method of comparing the standard of students in different years is to compare their performance on banked questions which more than one group have taken. If the whole test does not consist of questions used or pretested previously, then performance on individual banked questions must be compared by reference to the questions' analysis. If the two groups of students under consideration (i.e. this year's and those of a previous year) differ in their performance on questions which both groups took, then this shows a genuine difference in their standard of attainment. In an objective test it is known that the standard of the marking remains the same.

(e) If the whole test consists of questions which have been used or pretested previously, this will give an accurate picture of the standard of attainment of the students taking it relative to those in previous years.

Provided that security has been maintained there is no need to look for other evidence. Indeed, the pass mark can be set when the test is compiled (see Chapter 16) and need not be varied—if the marks obtained are not as expected, one can be sure that the difference genuinely lies with the students and not with the standard of the test.

Borderline Students

Since no subjective judgment is involved in the marking of objective tests, there is no point in reviewing the answers of borderline students (i.e. those just below the pass mark) from that point of view. However, the accuracy of the marking should be checked, in case there are any correct answers for which credit has not been given.

The results of students who are borderline on the objective paper may also be reviewed in the light of their performance on other components. If they have done well on other papers or assessments, an overall pass may be awarded despite their slight shortcomings on the objective paper. The combination of results of individual assessment components into an overall result is discussed in Book 1 of this series.

Special Cases

It may also be necessary to review the results of certain students who are 'special cases'; for example those who were affected at the time of the examination by illness, bereavement or serious domestic troubles. The final result of such students should be based as much on their performance during the course as on their answers to questions on the day. If the test under consideration is one of a series, the results on other tests in the series may be given greater weight when the overall result of such a 'special case' student is decided.

APPLICATION
1. List the factors taken into consideration when determining the pass mark for an objective test with which you are concerned.

2. What evidence, if any, is there to show that the pass mark used each year represents the same level of attainment?

3. What procedures are used for (a) borderlines and (b) special cases? Are they adequate?

PART V

Review and Banking

14

Review of the Test as a Whole

The examination or test should be reviewed, preferably before results are issued, to find out how well it has functioned. Usually a test review includes the review of individual questions, which is considered in the next chapter. In this chapter we concentrate on the review of the test as a whole, the aims of which are to provide information to assist in result determination; to provide information which will be helpful to examiners setting future tests; and (occasionally) to help identify whole tests suitable for banking. (Review of individual questions identifies those questions which may be banked.)

The review should be undertaken by two or three people who have been concerned with the production of the test, for example as writers or editors, and who are willing to learn from the results.

The review can take the form of asking and attempting to answer a number of questions concerning the performance of the test and of the students. Part of the information for answering these questions will come from statistical analysis or from simple numerical checks. The analysis required for the review of the test as a whole is quite easy to calculate; methods of calculation and worked examples are given in Appendix A.

The analysis should be regarded as a tool rather than as a master and should be only a part of the information considered. The reviewers should repeat the checks made at the compilation stage concerning such points as conformity to the specification (see Chapter 10) and should also take into account any comments received from students or other lecturers and (in the case of external examinations) comments received from other colleges.

The questions to be asked concerning the performance of the test as a whole are set out below.

1. Was the Time Allowed Adequate?

It is recommended (see Chapter 11) that students be asked to state at the end of the test how long they spent in answering the questions; it is then easy to summarise the information. Example 14.1 shows the information which might be obtained for a two-hour test taken by 50 students. It can be seen that all students finished the test in the time available and that most (70%) had finished by the end of one and a half hours. This is a fairly typical and quite satisfactory situation. It is better to allow too much time than too little, and only in extreme situations should a reduction in the time allowance be considered.

It is to be expected that in any test there will be only a handful of students (say less than 5%) who fail to finish. If more than 5% fail to finish, consideration should be given to extending the time allowance or reducing the number of questions in the test.

2. Did Most Students Attempt all Questions?

This is not quite the same as the question asked in Paragraph 1, although the two are obviously linked. A student may do all he can within the permitted time but still omit a number of questions because he is unable to answer them. Unless the analysis is provided by means of a computer program which specifically gives this information, the answer is likely to be found indirectly from an examination of the number of students who omitted to answer each individual question (see Chapter 15—Review of Individual Questions). It is not necessary to count manually the number of questions which each student attempted. There should not normally be more than about 5% of students

---

EXAMPLE

14.1   *Time Taken by Students to Complete Question Paper*

			Time Taken to complete				
	Under 1 hour	1-1 ¼ h	1 ¼ – 1 ½ h	1½ – 1 ¾ h	1 ¾ – 2 h	Not finished	Total
Number of students	4	15	16	13	2	0	50
Percent	8	30	32	26	4	0	100

omitting any particular question; if there are more than 5% then the question may be confusing or outside the syllabus. Several such questions in one test would reduce the reliability and validity of the test. The remedy would, however, lie in amending or replacing the individual questions.

3. Was the Average Performance Satisfactory?

The simplest indicator of the performance of students on a test is the mean (or average) of the marks they obtained. This may be expressed as a 'raw mark' (e.g. 48 out of 80) or as a percentage.

It may be expected that the percentage mean for a four-option multiple-choice test will be in the range 50—70%; the theoretical optimum is 62.5% which is half way between the 'chance score' (25%) and the maximum (100%). For a test of five-option questions, or one which included multiple-response or matching questions, a rather lower mean (down to 45% or even lower) could be acceptable. In any test both the mean and the pass mark should be well above the chance score, which is 25% for four-option questions, 20% for five-option and under 10% for most sorts of multiple-response and matching questions (see Chapter 4).

At the other end of the range, a mean above about 70% would indicate a test which was too easy for the level of student and therefore did not differentiate adequately between students of average attainment and those of high attainment. However, in some tests, the test constructors may not be interested in identifying the students of highest attainment, but in assessing the students' mastery of a body of knowledge or abilities; in such a test a mean around 70% would be acceptable.

If the mean mark on a test is higher than expected, the reason may be that the students were above the level of knowledge expected for the test or that the test itself was too easy; this in turn may result either from the content of the questions or from the use of a large number of weak distractors (see Paragraph 3, Chapter 15).

If the mean mark on a test is below what might be expected, the reason may be that:

(a) the test is too difficult;

(b) there are a large number of debatable or unclear questions;

(c) the time allowed was inadequate (see Paragraph 1);

(d) the students are below the standard which may be expected.

4. Was the Mean Mark Similar to that Obtained in Previous Years?

Unless the number of students is small, it can normally be expected that the mean mark on a test will remain broadly similar from year to year. If not, then it is necessary to ask whether the difference results from a difference in the standard of the test or in the ability of the students. This question was considered in Chapter 13—Result Determination. However, if the questions have been pretested and are known to be of equal difficulty, then it can be confidently stated that any differences are due to the students.

5. Did the Test Differentiate between Students of Different Ability?

It is generally best for a test to result in a fairly wide spread of marks, so as to differentiate between students of different ability. If the marks obtained are well spread out it is possible to separate the students who qualify for a higher grade of pass from the others, and to distinguish between the just-passes and the just-fails. If the marks obtained are all close together, then only a few marks separate students in different grades.

The following indicators of the spread of marks can be used:

(a) *The range* of marks states the bottom and top marks obtained on the test, e.g. 17 to 55 (out of 60). The range of marks on a test usually extends from just above the chance score to somewhere around 90%—it is rare for a student to score full marks. Although the range provides some information, it is not very helpful, because it does not show how the rest of the scores have been distributed. If the bottom mark is 17, the next may be 20 (as in Example 14.2) but could be 25 or 30.

(b) *A frequency distribution* shows the distribution of all of the marks obtained. Examples 14.2—14.4 are three frequency distributions, each for a test of 60 questions and each for around 80—90 students. Example 14.2 is a fairly typical distribution for a multiple-choice test, with the marks quite well spread out and extending from 17 (just above the chance score of 15) to 55. Example 14.3 shows the distribution for a rather easy test. The marks are concentrated in the upper part of the scale, with a long 'tail' at the bottom. This is known as a 'negatively skewed' distribution. Example 14.4 is rather more unusual; it has a main distribution extending down to 24 and a separate cluster of students near to 15, which is the chance

EXAMPLES

14.2–14.4 *Frequency Distributions for 60-question Tests*

	14.2	**14.3**	**14.4**
Mark	*Tally*	*Tally*	*Tally*
56			//
55	/		
54		/	/
53	/		
52			///
51		/	/
50	/	//	///
49	//	///	///
48		///	////
47	/	卌	/
46		卌 /	////
45	/	卌 ///	//
44		卌 卌	卌
43	///	卌 /	卌
42	//	卌 ////	////
41	//	卌 ///	///
40	/	卌 //	///
39	///	//	////
38	卌	///	卌
37	卌 /	//	///
36	卌	///	//
35	///	//	///
34	卌 /	/	///
33	////	//	////
32	卌		/
31	卌 ///	/	//
30	卌 /		/
29	////		
28	////	/	/
27	///		
26	卌	/	//
25	///	/	
24	/		/
23	//		
22	/	/	
21			
20	//		
19		/	
18		/	/
17	/		
16			//
15			
14			//
13			/
12			/

score. It may be that these were students who were totally unprepared for the test. Alternatively, it is possible that these are students from a quite different test, whose answer sheets happened to get mixed up with those from the test under consideration; since the order of the keys on the two tests is not the same, their apparent 'score' is close to the chance score. This is, of course, unusual, but it can happen, particularly where the marking is automatic; the inclusion of such answer sheets can seriously distort the analysis obtained.

(c) The *standard deviation* (or s.d.), often represented by the Greek lower case sigma (σ), is a single figure which indicates the spread of the marks on a test; the larger the standard deviation, the more the marks are spread. Unlike the range, the standard deviation takes into account all the marks obtained, but it does not show the shape of the distribution, so a frequency distribution is a useful adjunct.

A typical standard deviation for an objective test is 10—12% of the maximum possible mark. The standard deviation of the distribution shown in Example 14.2 is 7.25 out of 60 (12.08%). A standard deviation below 10% is undesirable, because it indicates an inadequate spread of marks. The σ of Example 14.3 is 6.51 (10.85%), which is not far above the minimum. There is no upper limit to the acceptable range of distribution provided that it does not result, as in Example 14.4, from the inclusion of some spurious students. The standard deviation of Example 14.4 is 10.08 (16.8%); if the spurious students are excluded, the σ of the remainder is 7.19 (11.98%).

If the standard deviation is below 10%, possible reasons are that:

(i)   the test is either too easy or too difficult (see Paragraph 3);
(ii) the students are genuinely very similar in their level of attainment;
(iii) the questions test different abilities and therefore do not all 'pull together' (see Paragraph 5, Chapter 15);
(iv) there are a number of poor questions with low discrimination (see Paragraph 5, Chapter 15).

6. Was the Paper Consistent in its Measurement?

The internal consistency of the test is indicated to some extent by the size of the standard deviation (see Paragraph 5(c) above) and by the discrimination indices of the individual questions (see Paragraph 5, Chapter 15). A single figure which summarises the test's internal consistency is the so-called 'reliability' coefficient (see Appendix A for method of calculation). This is a form of correlation coefficient, with possible values ranging up to 1.0. It should be noted that the only aspect of reliability which is shown by this figure is the test's internal consistency; it gives no information about, for example, the relative syllabus coverage and difficulty of this and other tests.

For a large national examination, a reliability figure above 0.8 is to be expected. For a smaller, college test, a rather lower figure would be expected and down to 0.75 would be acceptable. A pretest, which is likely to include a number of unsatisfactory questions, would give a lower figure. If the reliability is below the minimum desirable, this is very likely to be associated with a low standard deviation and the possible reasons are the same as those suggested above (Paragraph 5(c)) for a low σ.

APPLICATION

1. Review the results of a test with which you are concerned, by reference to:
   (a) time taken to answer;
   (b) mean mark;
   (c) standard deviation;
   (d) reliability.
   (See Appendix A for methods of calculation.)

2. What changes, if any, would you recommend for the test?

15

Review of Individual Questions

In Chapter 14 we outlined the points to be considered when reviewing the test as a whole. This chapter deals with the review of each of the individual questions, which is normally undertaken with the review of the whole test. The aims of the review of individual questions may include:

(a) shedding light on the behaviour of the test as a whole;

(b) enabling unsatisfactory questions to be excluded from the marking before the results are decided;

(c) providing information which will be of help in the setting of future papers;

(d) identifying questions suitable for banking and those which require modification before reuse.

As with the review of the whole paper, the review of individual questions may take the form of asking and attempting to answer a number of questions concerning the performance of students. The essential statistical analysis can be done with the help of a fairly simple calculator, although a semi-manual analysis will omit some of the details which can be provided by a computer program. Question analysis can provide very useful information concerning the performance of a question and should be taken seriously, but it should not be followed slavishly. Although analysis may suggest that there is something wrong with a question, it requires the judgment of a subject expert to say just what is wrong and how the question may be put right. The reviewers should review the text of the question, as well as the analysis, and should repeat the most important of the checks made at the editing stage, including confirming the correctness of the key.

The questions to be asked about each individual question during the review are set out below.

1. Did Most Students Attempt the Question?

The analysis should include counting and percentaging the number of students who failed to attempt the question (usually designated 'O' for 'omit'). Normally, each question should be attempted by at least 95% of students. If the percentage of omits is above five, possible reasons may be that:

(a) the question is at the end of a paper which has been shown to be too long (see Paragraph 1, Chapter 14);

(b) the topic is outside the syllabus;

(c) the topic is within the syllabus, but has not been taught, perhaps from lack of time (this is unlikely to happen throughout a national examination but could happen in a college exam);

(d) the question is too long or confusing;

(e) the question is actually wrong in some way, for example as the result of a misprint or of the omission of some necessary piece of information;

(f) the question is too difficult (see also Paragraph 2).

2. Was the Question of Appropriate Difficulty?

The answer to this question may be inferred from the 'facility', which is the percentage of the students taking the test who answered the question correctly; omits are counted as wrong when calculating facility. The facility of a question should normally be in the range 40—90.

A facility *above 90* indicates that the question was very easy and contributed little to the process of assessment. Occasionally such a question may be retained; for example if it concerns an important topic such as safety which is well-known but still needs to be tested. Otherwise it may be possible to improve the question by substituting better distractors (see Paragraph 3) or by rewriting it in conjunction with another topic (see Chapter 9, p. 127). However, there should be a minimum of questions with facilities above 90 in any one paper. Often such questions cannot be modified and have to be excluded from the bank.

A question with a facility *below 40* is clearly very difficult, particularly when it is considered that 25% of students can be expected to answer a four-option question correctly simply by chance. Although a question with low facility is not necessarily one on which there were more omits than usual, the possible reasons for a low facility are broadly the same as those for a high percentage of omits (see Paragraph 1). The rest of the question analysis, as described later in the chapter, can help to shed light on the reasons for the low facility.

A question with a facility below 40 *may* be acceptable, but only if the reviewers are satisfied that it is within the syllabus, fair, accurate and clearly presented, and if the discrimination is good (see Paragraph 5).

3. Were the Distractors Plausible but not Misleading?

Evidence concerning the performance of the distractors is found by counting and percentaging the number of students who chose each of the possible options. The way in which this information may be presented is shown in Examples 15.1 (four-option multiple-choice question) and 15.2 (six-option multiple-response question), including in each case the omits. The keys are marked with an asterisk.

EXAMPLES

15.1 *Responses to Four-option Multiple-choice Question*

Option	No. of students	%
(a)	24	8
(b)	92	29
(c)	35	11
*(d)	165	52
O	3	1

15.2 *Responses to Six-option Multiple-response Question*

Option	No. of students	%
(a)	23	12
*(b)	139	72
*(c)	167	87
(d)	19	10
*(e)	171	89
(f)	15	8
O	13	7
Facility	125	65

For a multiple-choice question, the facility is equal to the percentage of students who chose the key—52% in Example 15.1. The position in a multiple-response question is more complex, because a student who chooses one of the keys does not necessarily choose the others also. Thus, in Example 15.2, not all of the 72% who chose (b) have also chosen (c) and (e); in fact only 65% of students have chosen all three of the keys, as the separate facility entry shows. In other multiple-response questions the degree of mismatch may be greater.

A display similar to Example 15.1 may be prepared for assertion/reason questions.

In a matching question the number of possible combinations is too great for them to be analysed manually. Analysis by computer would be theoretically possible, but would be so detailed that it would be difficult to interpret and might well shed little extra light on the performance of the question.

A distractor should normally attract at least 5% of the students taking the test. Although the aim should not be to mislead the students unfairly, a distractor which gains less than 5% support is not fulfilling a useful function—it is failing to distract those students who do not know the answer and effectively reducing the number of options to three. Naturally, if 90% of students know the answer without a shadow of doubt, then the three distractors cannot attract 5% each. However, in a question of 90% facility, some of the 90% may be students who do not know the answer, but have guessed correctly. The provision of better distractors might draw them away from the key and make the question more difficult and more searching.

A distractor which is more popular than the key may well be unfairly misleading. This cannot easily be determined without an examination of the question itself and a knowledge of the ability of the students who selected the distractor (see Paragraph 4 below).

It is sometimes held that the three distractors in a four-option question should attract approximately equal numbers of students. Although this may be ideal it is not strictly necessary provided that all are adequately plausible.

4. Was the Key Chosen by the Better Students?

It is to be expected that the key of a satisfactory question will be selected by students who are more able than those who chose the distractors—their ability being judged by their performance on the test as a whole. Of course, if the whole test contained a large number of unsatisfactory questions, it would be a poor measure of their attainment, but the situation is rarely as bad as that.

There are three types of evidence which may be used, not all of them being needed together.

(a) The *mean mark for each option*. Example 15.3 gives a more detailed analysis of the multiple-choice question first shown as Example 15.1. The columns for number and percentage of students are the same as in Example 15.1. The next column, headed 'mean', shows the mean mark, on the test as a whole, of those students who chose each of the options, including omits. It shows, for example, that the students who selected (a) as the answer to this question had a mean mark of 54.7 on the test as a whole, those who chose (b) scored an average of 54.4 and so on. Those who correctly chose (d) had a mean of 59.0 on the test as a whole, higher than the mean for any of the distractors. This is as it should be.

The *mean-for-option* may be found for each option of a multiple-choice, multiple-response or assertion/reason question. For a matching question, where the number of possible combinations of answers is too large to

EXAMPLES

15.3 *More Detailed Analysis for Example 15.1*

Option	No. of students	%	Mean	LG%	UG%
(a)	24	8	54.7	9.2	4.6
(b)	92	29	54.4	40.2	23.0
(c)	35	11	56.3	10.3	9.2
*(d)	165	52	59.0	40.2	63.2
O	3	1	55.0	0	0

15.4 *Analysis for Matching Question*

	No. of students	%	Mean	LG%	UG%
Correct	163	85	47.7	70	96
Wrong	18	9	41.7	13	4
Omit	11	6	35.5	17	0

handle, it is possible to show only the mean for those answering the whole question correctly, those answering incorrectly and omits. This information is given in the mean column of Example 15.4, which relates to a matching question.

(b) The *percentage of the upper and lower groups* who answered correctly. The *upper* group comprises those students who scored highest on the test as a whole and the *lower* group those who scored lowest. It is usual to take the top 27% as the upper group and the bottom 27% as the lower group. This leaves a middle 46% who do not feature in this part of the analysis. The penultimate column of Example 15.3 shows what percentage of the lower group chose each of the options for this question; for instance 9.2% of the lower group chose (a) and 40.2% chose (b). The last column shows that 4.6% of the upper group chose (a) and 23% chose (b). These two columns support the evidence of the mean column that the question has worked quite well. The key (d) has been chosen by more upper group students than lower group and each of the distractors has proved more attractive to the lower group than to the upper group. If this were not the case then it could indicate that the question was in some way wrong or misleading. A distractor which has proved attractive to the upper group may perhaps be partially correct; a key which has attracted fewer of the upper group than of the lower may be not wholly correct, or perhaps the question has seemed to the upper group to be too easy or a 'trick' question.

Similar information is given in the last two columns of Example 15.4 showing that 96% of upper group students answered this matching question correctly, but only 70% of the lower group. Only 4% of the upper group answered it incorrectly, but 13% of the lower group answered wrongly and a further 17% omitted it.

Although the information about the upper and lower groups is very useful, it should not be given undue weight. Even if the total number of students for the test is 200, the number in each of the upper and lower groups is only 54, so a single student makes a difference of nearly 2%. For a total test population below about 40, the upper and lower group figures are probably not worth calculating, as each of the groups would comprise fewer than a dozen students. Both the mean and the upper and lower group figures are tedious to calculate if computer analysis is not available.

(c) A *matrix display* may be used to show the students' responses to each question if the analysis is being done manually. The matrix can be useful on its own, or can be used as a first stage in the calculation of other statistics. Example 15.5 is the matrix for a four-option multiple-choice question. Each stroke indicates the response of one student, plotted according to his or her mark on the paper as a whole and response to this question. Thus, the one student who scored 48 on the test as a whole chose (c) as the answer to this question. Of the six students who scored 44, one chose (a) and the remaining five chose (d).

Lines can be drawn to show the limits of the upper and lower groups; in this case the upper group has been taken as those scoring 37 or above on the test as a whole and the lower group as those scoring 29 or below. The

EXAMPLE

15.5 *Matrix Display for Multiple-choice Question*

Mark on whole test	Answers to Question 15				
	(a)	(b)	(c)	*(d)	O
48			/		
44	/			卌	
43	//		/	//	
42	/			//	
41	/				
40	/			////	
39	/	/		卌	/
38	///			卌	//
37	//			卌	///
				卌	卌
36	/	/	/	卌	/
35	///	/		卌	卌 //
34	卌			卌	//
33	卌 ///	///		//	///
32	////		/	////	
31	///			卌	
30	卌	/		卌	卌
29	///		/	卌	/
28	卌 /			///	
27	////			///	
26	//		/	//	
25	////			//	
24				//	
23	//		/	///	
22	//	/		/	
21				/	
20	/				
Total	66	4	9	114	0
%	34	2	5	59	0

display shows that on this question the lower group was largely divided between (a) and (d), but a higher proportion of the better students chose the key. This impression is confirmed if the mean and LG/UG figures are calculated, as in Example 15.6. This question would probably be considered acceptable, but it would be wise for the reviewers to look again at option (a) to determine why it proved so attractive, even to some of the better students. Also, distractor (b) is weak.

5. Did the Question Measure the Same Abilities as the Test as a Whole?

The simplest answer to this question is found in the *discrimination index,* which attempts to summarise in a single figure the information conveyed in the mean and LG/UG columns of the analysis. The discrimination index (D) is a correlation coefficient representing the degree of association between performance on the test as a whole and on the question under consideration.

The theoretical range of the discrimination index is from -1.0 to $+1.0$. A discrimination of $+1.0$ would indicate a perfect correlation between marks on the whole test and marks on the individual question, with all the better students getting the question right and all the poorer ones getting it wrong. A value of -1.0 would indicate the reverse situation, with the better students getting the question wrong and the poorer ones getting it right—a disastrous position. In practice neither of these two extremes is ever found. Most discrimination figures found in actual tests fall within the range 0 to $+0.45$. A question with a discrimination below 0, i.e. negative, should not be accepted into a question bank without modification and further testing; such a question should, if possible, be excluded from consideration when deciding

---

EXAMPLE

15.6 *Analysis for Example 15.5*

Option	%	Mean	LG%	UG%
(a)	34	31.53	47	24
(b)	2	33.0	2	2
(c)	5	33.67	6	4
*(d)	59	33.89	45	69
O	0			

students' results. A negative discrimination indicates that there is definitely something wrong with the question.

A value of D which is small but positive may sometimes be acceptable but may indicate that there is something amiss. The minimum value of D which can be considered acceptable depends upon the number of students and is discussed in Appendix B (p. 218). A figure of 0.2 is often regarded as the minimum acceptable, but this assumes that the number of students is in the range 150-200. The larger the number of students taking the test, the greater the reliance which may be placed on the discrimination figures obtained.

Of the examples of question analysis which we have considered earlier in the chapter, Example 15.3 has a D of 0.225 (number of students 319), Example 15.4 has a D of 0.33 (number of students 192) and Example 15.5 has a D of 0.18 (193 students); all these are acceptable, although that of Example 15.5 is only just so.

If the discrimination of a question is less than should be expected, then the possible reasons are that:

(a) the question is either too easy or too difficult; a question which is at either of these two extremes cannot discriminate well between different levels of student;

(b) the question is testing a different ability from that tested by the rest of the paper; this *may* be acceptable, but it is debatable whether the question should appear in the same paper;

(c) the question is outside the syllabus or on a topic which has not been taught (see Paragraphs 1 and 2);

(d) the question is confusing in its wording or presentation;

(e) the key is not wholly correct and/or one of the distractors is partially true;

(f) there is no correct answer;

(g) there are several correct answers.

If a question has poor or negative discrimination, the reasons may be sought in the question itself and in the answers to the questions in Paragraphs 3 and 4.

Examples of Question Analysis

Some examples of actual question analysis are discussed in the following paragraphs to illustrate how the analysis may be used to judge the worth of the question.

Most of the abbreviations used have already been explained. F stands for facility, D for discrimination and n for number of students for the test as a whole.

Example 15.7 is a very easy question, with poor discrimination. None of the distractors has worked very well, (b) being particularly weak. Although such a question might be retained if the topic were considered really important, it would be better if at least one of the distractors could be replaced by something more plausible. Certainly one would not wish to include more than one or two such questions in a single test.

Example 15.8 has produced generally good results. The facility and discrimination are well within the acceptable range, the mean and upper group percentage are higher for the key than for the distractors and the distractors were more popular with the lower than with the upper group. However, option (c) is a very weak distractor, attracting only 1% of students, and should be replaced by something more plausible.

Example 15.9 is rather difficult—somewhat surprisingly in view of the subject matter of the question. However, in other respects the question has proved satisfactory and it has discriminated well, so it would be considered acceptable.

EXAMPLE

15.7 *Food Service*

The main criteria of an à la carte menu are that the dishes are:
(a)   cooked to order and individually priced
(b)   specialities of the house served on a call order system
(c)   cooked to order and priced on an inclusive basis
(d)   prepared in advance and individually priced.

Option	No. of students	%	Mean	LG%	UG%		
*(a)	173	92	51.3	88.5	94.2	n	189
(b)	3	2	52.3	1.9	3.8	F	91.5
(c)	8	4	45.5	7.7	1.9	D	0.081
(d)	5	3	51.2	1.9	0		
O	0						

Example 15.10 is not quite as difficult as Example 15.9 but has not discriminated at all well. The mean for (a) is higher than for the key and (a) proved very attractive to the better students. The reviewers of this question decided that the key was not correct—the answer should be five minutes, which explains the popularity of option (a). The options were therefore adjusted accordingly.

Example 15.11 was both difficult and of low discrimination. From the mean and LG and UG columns it can be seen that the main reason was the popularity of option (c), even with the better students. One possible cause of the difficulty was that many people (including, it appears, many of these students)

EXAMPLES

15.8 *Cookery*

Brown beef stock reduced to a thick substance is called:
(a) extract
(b) jelly
(c) emulsion
(d) glaze.

Option	No. of students	%	Mean	LG%	UG%		
(a)	54	21	49.1	29.2	12.5	n	263
(b)	12	5	47.8	9.7	1.4	F	73.8
(c)	3	1	47.3	1.4	0	D	0.238
*(d)	194	74	53.0	59.7	86.1		
O	0						

15.9 *Food Service*

How should teaspoons be washed?
(a)   in cutlery racks in a dishwashing machine.
(b)   in a jug of very hot water by the food server at the sideboard.
(c)   in a bowl of hot water by the still-room attendant.
(d)   in the burnishing machine by the plate room attendant.

Option	No. of students	%	Mean	LG%	UG%		
*(a)	72	38	54.4	26.9	63.5	n	189
(b)	21	11	48.3	15.4	3.8	F	38.1
(c)	76	40	49.8	38.5	28.8	D	0.327
(d)	19	10	47.2	17.3	3.8		
O	1	1	43.0	1.9	0		

are more familiar with a pear condé which does include fruit. In order to overcome this difficulty the reviewers reworded the question to refer to the base for a fruit condé. A question with results of this sort would not be acceptable for banking without amendment.

At first sight Example 15.12 appears quite unacceptable, much too difficult and with negative discrimination. However, the key is incorrectly marked and the analysis has been calculated on the basis of the wrong key. If the analysis is recalculated with (c) as the key, the facility becomes 73 and the discrimination 0.13. The discrimination is still too low for ready acceptance, and (d) is a weak distractor. Replacing (d) with a more plausible option might also make the question a little more discriminating.

EXAMPLES

15.10 *Cookery*

The time taken to cook frozen peas after their immersion in boiling water is:
(a) 3 minutes
(b) 7 minutes
(c) 10 minutes
(d) 17 minutes.

Option	No. of students	%	Mean	LG%	UG%		
(a)	93	29	58.9	23.0	41.4	n	319
*(b)	132	41	57.5	39.1	41.4	F	41.4
(c)	78	24	54.9	29.9	14.9	D	0.042
(d)	16	5	52.8	8.0	2.3		
O	0						

15.11 *Cookery*

A rice condé consists of rice cooked in milk and:
(a) sugar, egg yolks and flavouring
(b) crystallised fruits, gelatine, cream and sugar
(c) fresh fruits, gelatine, cream and sugar
(d) sugar, egg yolks, flavouring and egg whites.

Option	No. of students	%	Mean	LG%	UG%		
*(a)	91	29	57.5	26.4	29.9	n	319
(b)	31	10	55.4	10.3	6.9	F	28.5
(c)	154	48	58.2	41.4	57.5	D	0.031
(d)	43	13	53.2	21.8	5.7		
O	0						

Example 15.13 is a multiple-response question which has proved much too difficult and has discriminated hardly at all. Examination of the figures for the options shows that two factors have contributed to this. Option (b), which was one of the keys, was chosen by only 32% of the students, although those who did know it were amongst the better students (their mean on the whole test was higher than the mean for any of the other options). The second factor was that option (d) proved very popular, especially with the better students. In fact, some tutors stated that this was a possible correct answer, and therefore inadmissible as a distractor. In order to remedy the question it would, therefore, be necessary to replace (d) by a wrong but plausible distractor. This might cause some of the students to choose (b) instead, but the question would probably still be very difficult. Only further pretesting could determine whether it would be acceptable after this modification.

Example 15.14 is a multiple-response question which has worked much better; both the facility and the discrimination are within the expected range. Option (d) has proved slightly more popular with the upper group than with the lower, but this is not significant as it is in fact a difference of only two students. The only modification to be made to the question, if possible, is that option (b) should be replaced.

Example 15.15 shows the results of an assertion/reason question. Although this is only slightly too difficult, it has not discriminated at all well and would

---

EXAMPLES

15.12 *Cookery*

The most suitable method of cooking ox liver would be:
(a) grilling
(b) shallow frying
(c) braising
(d) griddling.

Option	No. of students	%	Mean	LG%	UG%		
(a)	10	4	47.9	4.2	0	n	263
*(b)	51	19	51.4	25.0	20.8	F	19.4
(c)	193	73	52.5	65.3	77.8	D	−0.034
(d)	7	3	49.6	2.8	1.4		
O	2	1	40.0	2.8	0		

EXAMPLES

15.13 *Practical Nursing*

Which FOUR of the following items of information are relevant in helping the nurse prepare the bed area for a patient being admitted as an emergency?
(a) the patient's state of consciousness
(b) whether the patient is being admitted from home or the street
(c) whether the patient is in a state of shock
(d) the patient's age
(e) whether relatives are accompanying the patient
(f) whether the patient is in severe pain.

Option	No. of students	%	Mean	LG%	UG%		
all correct	30	16	47.2	17	13		
*(a)	186	97	46.5	93	100	n	192
*(b)	62	32	48.7	28	38	F	16
*(c)	177	92	46.9	83	98	D	0.04
(d)	128	67	47.2	57	78		
(e)	25	13	44.4	20	9		
*(f)	144	75	46.3	74	73		

15.14 *Practical Nursing*

Which TWO of the following observations would be *most* likely to indicate that a patient's fluid intake is inadequate?
(a) the patient has a dirty mouth
(b) the patient has developed oedema
(c) the patient is on diuretics
(d) the patient is very drowsy
(e) the patient's urine is very concentrated
(f) the patient is pyrexial.

Option	No. of students	%	Mean	LG%	UG%		
all correct	124	65	48.33	54	84		
*(a)	129	67	48.04	59	85	n	192
(b)	3	2	37.67	4	0	F	65
(c)	10	5	42.4	7	2	D	0.28
(d)	22	11	46.41	6	9		
*(e)	180	94	47.11	81	100		
(f)	24	13	41.44	19	4		
O	8	4	36.0	11	0		

not normally be acceptable without modification. The reasons for the question's poor performance are not completely clear, and it may well be that it had not been taught or was outside the scope of the students' knowledge and experience. However, it can be inferred from the analysis that the

EXAMPLES

15.15 *Psychology for Nurses*

ASSERTION
Emotional maturity is an ideal and not a state which many people ever reach

BECAUSE

REASON
most children suffer some emotional trauma in the course of growing up.

With reference to the above, which of the following is correct?

(a) Both assertion and reason are true statements and the reason is a correct explanation of the assertion.

(b) Both assertion and reason are true statements but the reason is not a correct explanation of the assertion.

(c) The assertion is true but the reason is a false statement.

(d) The assertion is false, but the reason is a true statement.

(e) Both assertion and reason are false statements.

Option	%	Mean	LG%	UG%		
(a)	13	43.23	14	16		
*(b)	39	44.2	29	36	n	100
(c)	14	42.71	11	4	F	39
(d)	22	41.05	36	24	D	0.08
(e)	8	41.25	11	8		
O	4	56.5	0	12		

15.16 *Psychology for Nurses*

Match the names of psychologists in List 1 with the contribution each has made to the understanding of child development, as given in List 2.

List 1	List 2
(A) Gesell	(1) carried out experiments in conditioning of dogs
(B) Pavlov	(2) identified developmental tasks
(C) Erikson	(3) tried to identify developmental norms
(D) Piaget	(4) was concerned with cognitive development of the child
	(5) tried to list human instincts.

	%	Mean	LG%	UG%		
Correct	17	47.8	7	28	n	100
Wrong	82	42.5	93	72	F	17
Omit	1	42	0	0	D	0.26

problem was not with the reason. Options (c) and (e) were together chosen by a total of only 22% of students, indicating that the remainder knew the reason to be a true statement. The 22% of students who chose (d) thought the assertion to be false and a wording of 'complete emotional maturity' might be preferable.

Example 15.16 shows the analysis for a matching question. This has discriminated adequately, but was too difficult. Some of the difficulty probably stems from the need for students to know all four items in the question in order to gain a mark. The question might well be fairer, as well as easier, if it were rewritten as a multiple-choice question asking for the contribution of only one of the psychologists (see Chapter 8).

APPLICATION

1. Calculate the analysis for some questions of a test which you set, or with which you are concerned. Include multiple-choice, multiple-response, assertion/reason and matching questions as appropriate. (See Appendices B and C for methods of calculation.)

2. Use the analysis and the recommendations of this chapter to review these questions. What modifications to the questions would you suggest?

16

Pretesting, Banking and Test Compilation from Banked Questions

This chapter describes the procedures involved in question banking and the associated tasks of pretesting and examination or test compilation. Example 16.1 lists the stages involved in setting up and operating a bank, working from the syllabus or course objectives. It is, of course, quite possible to analyse and bank examination questions without first pretesting and this may often be necessary in a single-college examination; Stages 8 to 12 would then be omitted.

EXAMPLE

16.1   *Procedures for Setting up a Bank*

(1)   Decide question type and examination conditions.
(2)   Prepare specification.
(3)   Train writers and editors.
(4)   Allocate question writing.
(5)   Write questions.
(6)   Edit questions.
(7)   Feedback to writers.
(8)   Compile pretests.
(9)   Hold pretests.
(10) Mark and analyse pretests.
(11) Review results.
(12) Bank satisfactory questions; revise unsatisfactory questions and hold for further pretesting.
(13) Compile examination or test.
(14) Mark, analyse and review questions.
(15) Update bank records.

Repeat stages 4 to 15 for subsequent pretests and examinations.

Why Pretest?

Before the first examination, a pretest is useful to establish the general suitability of the test or examination, the appropriateness of the questions overall and the adequacy of the time allowed. The first pretest also serves to test the suitability of the individual questions and this is the main function of subsequent pretests. After pretesting, the questions are analysed and reviewed to assess their difficulty, discriminating power and the plausibility of the distractors (see Chapter 15 on review of individual questions). This is necessary because it is often difficult to judge how an objective question will perform in practice. If a faulty constructed-answer question appears in an examination it may be possible to make corrections during marking; this is not possible with an objective question and the only course of action is then to omit that question from the result calculations.

Pretesting is also a useful, though not essential, preliminary to establishing a bank of questions, the advantages of which are summarised later in this chapter.

Full-scale pretesting to give meaningful statistical analysis requires a sample size of around 250 students. However, if these numbers are not available, it can still be useful to pretest with fewer. Even a pretest on 50 students could be useful in highlighting serious ambiguities in the questions or weak distractors.

Pretesting Procedures

The following points should be noted:

(a) The pretest should be compiled in accordance with the examination specification wherever possible. However, when a scheme has been running for a few years it may be found that the bank is weak in certain areas and it is then possible to weight the pretest in favour of those areas in order to restore the balance of the bank.

(b) The pretest should be taken under examination conditions.

(c) The students who take the pretest must have covered all the necessary subject matter in order to be as similar as possible to the students who will take the actual examination. In practice, this usually means that the pretest is held shortly before the students take their examination. This has the advantage that the students can use it as a 'trial run' and are therefore more motivated to take the pretest seriously.

(*d*) The students do not of course meet the same questions in the examination as in the pretest. In any case, if the preceding paragraph is followed, there would not be time to review the pretest results and compile an actual paper in the one or two weeks between pretest and examination. If the examination is an annual one, this year's pretest questions may, if suitable, form the basis for next year's examination.

(*e*) If possible, a sample of around 250 students should be used (see above).

(*f*) The sample of students taking the pretest should be representative of those who will take the examination; thus, if more than one college is concerned with the examination, students of more than one college should take the pretest. In a large national examination the pretest will need to include some students from each region, some from large colleges and some from small and so on.

(*g*) The security of the questions must be maintained, so papers must be collected after the test.

(*h*) Results of the pretest do not contribute to the students' examination result, but it is courteous to inform the students and their lecturers how they have fared.

Assisting an External Examining Body with Pretesting

Colleges are often asked to assist external examining bodies by arranging pretests; indeed their cooperation is essential to the pretesting and hence important for the validity and reliability of the examination. In order that their assistance is of most value, the college staff should ensure that:

(*a*) the students are on the course and at the level for which the pretest and examination are intended;

(*b*) the students have covered the necessary subject matter;

(*c*) the students are not totally unfamiliar with objective testing—at the very least they should have tried out a few questions and had instruction in the use of the answer sheet if one is used;

(*d*) the students are encouraged to do their best.

College staff are usually invited to comment on the pretest and their comments are taken into consideration when the results of the pretest are reviewed. It is important to remember that specific comments are likely to be more helpful than general ones. It is not easy for the examining body to take action on a comment such as 'Too many questions are debatable'; it is much more informative to be told 'In Question 21 either (a) or (b) could be a possible answer'. However, it may be helpful, particularly if the test is a recently introduced one, to give a general comment as well; for example 'The test as a whole was too difficult/too easy/satisfactory/too long/too short'. Comments on individual questions should be given in question order. To be of any value at all the comments must of course be legible!

Why Bank?

Even if pretesting is not feasible, the questions used in the examinations or tests should be analysed to judge their suitability (see Chapter 15) and satisfactory ones should be banked. The use of a bank of questions has the following advantages:

(a) Good questions are retained and reused, so improving the overall quality of the test.

(b) Resources are used more efficiently; much care and trouble goes, or should go, into the setting of an objective question and it is wasteful to discard this after one use.

(c) Most courses contain some topics which must be tested regularly; there is little point in trying to set a new question to test the same knowledge and abilities if one already exists.

(d) Banking and reuse of questions enables the standard of the examination to be kept constant from year to year. Without a banking system it is impossible to be sure whether a drop in the pass rate results from a more difficult examination paper or a real fall in the standard of the students. With a bank it is possible to compare the results of this year's students with those of previous years by reference to common questions taken by both groups.

(e) The use of a bank makes possible more flexible examination arrangements, for example more frequent examinations, examinations on demand and greater freedom in the use of in-course tests.

Disadvantages of Banking

Question banking does have some disadvantages, although the advantages outweigh the drawbacks:

(a) The questions must be kept secure; papers must be collected in after the examination or test, and past papers cannot be made available to students or lecturers; sample papers should, however, be available.

As the size of the bank increases, security becomes less important, but it is always a significant factor where application questions are concerned; if an application question becomes known and the answer remembered, it is no longer application but factual recall.

(b) There is an initial capital outlay in setting up the bank and in holding both a pretest and an examination in the first year. In subsequent years the burden of setting questions may actually be slightly less than for a traditional system (particularly if more than one examination per year is required), but additional work is required on bank administration and record-keeping.

(c) There is some wastage of questions. Questions may fail to survive the pretest or may reach the bank and never be used in an actual examination. Questions may also become out of date and the bank contents must be reviewed periodically to check for this.

Bank Organisation

The procedures involved in setting up and operating a bank were listed in Example 16.1. Most of these have been discussed in more detail elsewhere in the book. For example, specifications were discussed in Chapter 6 and editing in Chapter 10.

The bank should be arranged according to the specification, with a separate section for each syllabus topic and for each ability tested. Each question should be typed or copied onto a separate card, with all the relevant information concerning its characteristics and use, i.e.

(a) the course, or unit and level, as appropriate;

(b) question reference number;

(c) the syllabus section;

(d) the ability tested;

(e) text of the question;

(f) key or keys;

(g) dates of pretest and of use, including incorporation in any test not yet held;

(h) analysis for each use.

If the question is part of a question 'group', this should be indicated and it is best to file the questions in each group together, even if they relate to different syllabus sections; there may be a separate bank section for question groups. It is also useful to record, on the bank card for each question, the reference numbers of any other questions with which it is 'incompatible', i.e. with which it overlaps in content, or to which it gives the answer.

Example 16.2 shows a bank card with the question and the associated information.

Modern technology offers the national body, and even the individual college, the possibility of computerised question banking, computer-assisted paper compilation and electronically controlled storage and printing of the text of the questions, for example by the use of a word-processor.

Compiling a Test or Examination from a Bank

Once the bank has been established it can be used to compile examination papers or tests of good quality and consistent standard. A question which has

---

EXAMPLE

16.2 *Contents of a Bank Card*

Subject: Basic Cookery   Bank accession number: 10
Syllabus section: 3   Ability: recall   Key: c

The country of origin of blue Stilton cheese is:

(a)   Denmark
(b)   Italy
(c)   England
(d)   France.

Pretest: May 1978   Used:

F   60.5   D   0.264

	No. of students	%	Mean	LG%	UG%
(a)	71	22	54.5	29.9	11.5
(b)	17	5	57.3	6.9	5.7
*(c)	193	61	59.0	43.7	77.0
(d)	38	12	51.8	19.5	5.7
O	0	0			

(Space provided for details of subsequent use, including analysis)

been accepted into the bank should not need further editing at compilation stage—indeed, changing the wording in more than the most minor way may affect the difficulty of the question. Only occasionally may there be some query as to the suitability of the question itself (see (*j*) below). The points to be observed when compiling a paper or test from banked questions are listed below. Some of these, (*a*) to (*d*), apply whether or not the questions have been pretested and banked; these are listed only briefly as they were discussed in Chapter 10. The remaining points (*e*) to (*k*), apply only if the questions have been pretested or used previously.

(*a*) The test must conform to the specification.

(*b*) The test must follow any other constraints which have been imposed, relating for example to the number of graphical or calculations questions or the number of non-multiple-choice questions to be used.

(*c*) One question should not overlap with, or answer, another.

(*d*) There should be no discernible pattern in the distribution of the keys.

(*e*) The test should not include too many questions which were used in the last test; the maximum proportion of such questions should be around 20%.

(*f*) The predicted mean for the test should be in the range 50—70%, preferably close to the 'ideal mean' which is 62.5% for four-option multiple-choice questions (see Paragraph 3, Chapter 14). This means that the average facility of the questions used should be in the range 50—70%. See Appendix A for the method of calculating the predicted mean.

(*g*) It is usually desirable, although some authorities disagree on this, to have a range of facility values so that there are some fairly easy questions and some fairly difficult. The use of questions of very high discrimination and near-identical facility would tend to polarise students into two groups, not necessarily in the desired proportions.

(*h*) The easiest questions should be at the beginning of the paper, to give the students confidence; the most difficult should be at the end. For medium-difficulty questions arrangement by topic is preferable, although topics whose questions are easier than average should come earlier in the paper than more difficult ones.

(*i*) The predicted standard deviation of the test should, if possible, be above 12% (see Appendix D for method of estimating σ). In practice this means that the average discrimination of the questions used should be above 0.24.

(*j*) The questions should be inspected to ensure that none of them has become out of date (see also (*b*) of Bank Audit below).

(*k*) The bank cards should be marked to show the date of the test in which each question is to be used—this information may be needed if a new test is to be compiled before the analysis for the current one is available to add to the bank cards.

The compilation of the paper should be done topic by topic; only as a last stage at the end are the questions rearranged according to their facility. If the bank is restricted in size or weak in some areas, it is a good idea to begin compilation with the areas which are weakest. If there are, for example, only four application questions on a particular topic in the bank and two are required for the test, then the compiler will wish to choose at least one of the two questions not used in the last previous test. He or she should then turn to the comprehension and recall questions for the same topic. Here, some questions may be excluded because of similarity in subject matter with the application questions already selected; others may be excluded in order not to have too many which have just been used. The choice between the remainder may be affected by their facility and discrimination; for example, if the chosen application questions are particularly difficult they should be balanced by relatively easy questions for the other abilities; if they are not very discriminating, the next questions chosen should be of above-average discrimination. When the questions from the weakest bank section have been chosen, the compiler may move to the next weakest section or to a related topic. It is wise to keep a running check on the average facility and discrimination of the questions chosen; a pocket calculator can help in this.

A second person should check the compilation to ensure that it complies with all the points listed above. It is also most important that a second person should check the list of keys and this should be done by reading the questions, not checking from a master list of keys.

Points to note concerning the layout and printing of the test were given in Chapter 11.

Bank Audit

The contents of the bank should be reviewed periodically (say every three years) by a subject expert, possibly assisted by an administrator—this may be termed a *bank audit*. The auditors should check that:

(a) there are no overworked questions; these should be discarded. In general a question which has been used in four or more main examination series should be considered for exclusion. It may be possible to write an alternative question testing the same topic and ability using the techniques outlined in Chapter 9 (pp. 129—33).

(b) there are no out-of-date questions. This may occur as a result of changes in technology or industrial practice. Thus, Example 16.3, which was designed to test whether students could recognise a digital display, was written at a time when (b) was the only likely answer. Now, however, (c) or (d) could also have a digital display, so the question is no longer valid.

(c) questions which overlap or answer one another are marked as incompatible.

(d) the percentage of the bank questions in each 'cell' (i.e. each topic and ability) is approximately in proportion to the percentage required for that cell by the specification. If some cells are found to be particularly weak, the next round of writing, editing and pretesting should concentrate on those areas.

(e) the bank administration has been correct; for example that all questions are filed in the correct place and that there are full records of all uses of the questions, including analysis.

Lecturers concerned with more than one course, or colleagues concerned with similar courses, may be able to reduce duplication of effort by cross-referencing questions which are appropriate to more than one course or unit. Usually this involves reading through all the questions in one bank (or in the relevant parts of the bank) to identify those which are suitable for another course; a second bank card should be made for use in the second bank, and both cards should carry information about the cross-referencing. Sometimes the requirements of the two courses are different enough to affect the

---

EXAMPLE

16.3 *Electrical Control*

Which of the following has a digital display?
(a) a car tachometer
(b) a car odometer
(c) a watch
(d) supermarket scales.

performance of the questions; thus the facility of the question may be much higher for the students in one course than for those in another.

APPLICATION

1. Are there any objective tests with which you are concerned which do not have question banking?

   (a) How would the introduction of banking improve the reliability and efficiency of the tests?

   (b) What extra work would be involved?

2. Review the banking arrangements for an existing bank.

   (a) Is pretesting undertaken? If not, would it be feasible?

   (b) What measures are taken to ensure that the pretests are representative and secure?

   (c) What analysis is obtained from the pretest and examination? Could more useful analysis be obtained? Is the analysis used when compiling tests?

   (d) Is the bank arranged in the best possible way? Are all the questions correctly filed and accompanied by all relevant information?

   (e) Check the compilation of a recent test drawn from the bank. Does it conform to all the recommendations of this chapter?

   (f) Has the bank been audited recently? If not, undertake an audit, following the recommendations of this chapter.

PART VI

Appendices

The appendices describe, with worked examples, the calculations required for the analysis of the results of the whole test (Appendix A) and of individual multiple-choice and other objective questions (B and C), and for predicting the statistics for a test compiled from banked questions (D). Appendix E lists, for ease of reference, the statistical notation used.

It is assumed that at least a basic electronic calculator is available; the calculator chosen should have an accumulating memory and a square root key. It is also possible to obtain statistical calculators pre-programmed to calculate mean and standard deviation, and these considerably reduce the work involved. It should be noted, however, that such calculators may be programmed to use $(n - 1)$ instead of n in standard deviation calculations, giving a slightly larger result. They may also be limited in the number of items of data they can accept in one calculation.

The stages of the calculations are described in some detail in the appendices and readers will probably find they can take short cuts, at least when they are familiar with the procedure — for example using a calculator with a memory makes it unnecessary to write down all the figures obtained in intermediate stages of the calculation.

The use of electronic calculators makes it unnecessary to use the approximate methods which were recommended in the past, for example the upper group/lower group method of calculating discrimination, although this has been included for information.

It is assumed throughout these appendices that the method of scoring is to award one mark for each question answered completely correctly.

A

Calculating the Statistics for the Test as a Whole

Frequency Distribution

A frequency distribution is of value in itself because it gives an indication of the way in which the marks obtained have been distributed (see Chapter 14, p. 172). It is also a useful first stage in the calculation of the mean and standard deviation, if a programmed calculator is not available. The scripts or answer sheets should already have been marked, but the marks should *not* be converted to a percentage. It is of some advantage to sort the scripts into rank order, if this is allowed, with the highest scoring scripts first. Columns 1 and 2 of Example A1 show the frequency distributions for a 60-question test taken by 92 students. Column 1 shows the marks obtained on the whole test, designated x_T (the subscript $_T$ indicates that these are marks for the whole test not for individual questions). Column 2 shows the frequency (f), the number of students who obtained that mark. Each student is indicated by a stroke (/) against the appropriate mark; the fifth occurrence of a particular mark is shown by a diagonal across the preceding four, making a 'gate' (卅); the tenth is shown by a diagonal in the opposite direction (卅). Thus the frequency distribution shows that only one student scored 55 on the whole test, two scored 49, five scored 38 and so on.

Mean

For fairly large numbers of students use the frequency distribution to find the mean. First complete Column 3 (fx_T). This gives the mark multiplied by the number of students who obtained that mark. For example, two students scored 49 and $2 \times 49 = 98$. Then add the fx_T column to give Σfx_T. The symbol Σ (Greek capital sigma) means 'sum of' and occurs again in other calculations.

The mean for the test, M_T, is found from the formula

$$M_T = \frac{\Sigma f\, x_T}{n_T}$$

where

x_T is the mark obtained by each student on the test,
$\Sigma f x_T$ is the sum of these marks and
n_T is the number of students taking the test.

EXAMPLE

A1   *Calculation of Mean and Standard Deviation*

1	2	3	4	5
Score	Tally			
x_T	f	fx_T	$x_T{}^2$	$fx_T{}^2$
55	/	55	3025	3025
53	/	53	2809	2809
50	/	50	2500	2500
49	//	98	2401	4802
47	/	47	2209	2209
45	/	45	2025	2025
43	///	129	1849	5547
42	//	84	etc.	3528
41	//	82		3362
40	/	40		1600
39	///	117		4563
38	/// /	190		7220
37	/// / /	222		8214
36	/// /	180		6480
35	///	105		3675
34	/// / /	204		6936
33	////	132		4356
32	/// /	160		5120
31	/// / ///	248		7688
30	/// / /	180		5400
29	////	116		3364
28	////	112		3136
27	///	81		2187
26	/// /	130		3380
25	///	75		1875
24	/	24		576
23	//	46		1058
22	/	22		484
20	//	40		800
17	/	17		289
Totals	92	3084		108 208

In Example A1

$$M_T = \frac{3084}{92}$$

$$= 33.52.$$

This is the 'raw score' mean out of the total available for the test (in this case 60). If necessary, the mean can be converted to a percentage by multiplying by $100/k$, where k is the number of question in the test. In Example A1 the percentage mean is

$$\frac{33.52 \times 100}{60} = 55.87.$$

If the number of students is quite small, their marks can be added all together without first multiplying (i.e. 55 + 50 + 49 + 49 etc.). The use of a $\Sigma f x_T$ column is generally quicker for larger numbers of students. In either case the end result is the same.

Standard Deviation

To find the standard deviation, working from the frequency distribution, it is necessary first to square each mark, to give $x_T{}^2$ (as shown in Column 4 of Example A1) and then to multiply each square by the number of students, to give $f x_T{}^2$ (as in Column 5). Thus $55^2 = 3025$ and only one student scored 55; $49^2 = 2401$ and this is multiplied by two (= 4802) because two students scored 49. Column 4 has not been completed in full because it is possible to find $f x_T{}^2$ on a calculator without the need to write down $x_T{}^2$; indeed, it is usually possible to put the $f x_T{}^2$ values into an accumulating memory, making it unnecessary to write down all the values in Column 5. When Column 5 has been worked out, it is added (or the calculator memory read) to give the sum of squares $\Sigma f x_T{}^2$. The standard deviation of marks for the test σ_T is then found from

$$\sigma_T = \sqrt{\frac{\Sigma f x_T{}^2 - n_T M_T{}^2}{n_T}}$$

where

x_T is the mark of each student,
$\Sigma f x_T{}^2$ is the sum of squares of these marks,
M_T is the mean for the test and
n_T is the number of students.

In Example A 1

$$\sigma_T = \sqrt{\frac{108\,208 - (92 \times 33.52^2)}{92}}$$
$$= 7.25.$$

This is the 'raw' standard deviation which 'like the mean' may be converted to a percentage if required.

Note

The formula for the standard deviation is often quoted as

$$\sigma_T = \sqrt{\frac{\Sigma d^2}{n_T}}$$

where

d is the difference of each mark from the mean,
Σd^2 is the sum of squares of these differences and
n_T is the number of students.

Using this formula has the advantage that smaller figures are involved, but the disadvantages that:

(a) an extra stage is involved because each mark must be subtracted from the mean before squaring;

(b) if the mean is not a whole number, it is necessary to round off, with slight loss of accuracy, or to work with one or two decimal places;

(c) it does not provide automatically the sum of squares, $\Sigma f x_T^2$, which is needed if two sets of marks are to be combined and the overall standard deviation found.

Reliability

For an accurate calculation of the reliability, r, of a test, Kuder–Richardson formula 20 should be used.

$$r = \frac{k}{k-1} \left(1 - \frac{\Sigma pq}{\sigma_T^2}\right)$$

where

k is the number of questions in the test,

p is the proportion of students passing a question (equal to the facility divided by 100),

q is $1 - p$

Σpq is the sum of the pq products for all questions and

σ_T is the test standard deviation.

Example A2 shows part of the calculation for an 80-question test which has a mean of 46.88 and a standard deviation of 10.32. For Question 1, F is 89, so p is 0.89 and q is 0.11; pq is 0.10. The pq values are found for each of the 80 questions and added to give Σpq. Then the reliability may be found by substituting in the formula

$$r = \frac{80}{79} \left(1 - \frac{17.32}{10.32^2} \right)$$
$$= 0.85.$$

If the facilities of the questions in the test are all fairly close, it is possible to use the more approximate formula, Kuder–Richardson 21,

$$r = \frac{k}{k-1} \left(1 - \frac{M_T (k - M_T)}{k\sigma_T^2} \right)$$

where

k is the number of questions in the test,

M_T is the test mean and

σ_T is the test standard deviation.

EXAMPLE

A2   *Calculation of reliability*

Question	F	pq
1	89	0.10
2	88	0.11
3	74	0.19
. . . .	. . . .	. . . .
80	34	0.22
Total		17.32

In Example A2

$$r = \frac{80}{79} \left(1 - \frac{46.88 \, (80 - 46.88)}{80 \times 10.32^2} \right)$$
$$= 0.83$$

If the number of questions were smaller or the spread of facilities greater, there might be a larger difference between this and the reliability found by formula 20.

B

Analysing Individual Multiple-choice Questions

The first stage in analysing a multiple-choice question without the aid of a computer is to prepare a matrix display, as shown in Example B1. The left column (x_T) shows the score on the whole test and the (a) to O columns show the responses given to the question under consideration. Each student's response to the question is shown by a stroke in the appropriate position. Thus, the only student to score 48 on the test as a whole chose (a) as the answer to this question. Of four students who scored 40 on the whole test, three chose (a) and one omitted the question and therefore appears in the O column.

As well as being a first stage in the calculation of the analysis, this matrix gives a visual display of how the question has performed. It can be seen that almost all the better students chose the correct answer (a)—indicated by an asterisk; many of the poorer students chose a distractor, notably (d).

Facility

The facility of the question is found by first counting the number of students who chose the correct answer, in this case (a). The facility F is then found from

$$F = \frac{n_p \times 100}{n_T}$$

where
n_p is the number of students who answered correctly and
n_T is the total number of students for the test.

In Example B1

$$F = \frac{64 \times 100}{116}$$
$$= 55.2.$$

Distractor Plausibility

To find how plausible each distractor proved, simply count the number of students who selected it. This may then be converted to a percentage. In Example B1, nine out of a total of 116 students chose (b). The percentage choosing (b) is therefore

$$\frac{9 \times 100}{116} = 7.8\%.$$

The same procedure is followed for the other distractors and for the omits.

Mean-for-option

The mean-for-option, which is frequently provided in computer analysis of multiple-choice questions, is not really essential if the analysis has to be done manually. If required, however, it may be found by adding the scores on the test as a whole of the students who chose each option and then dividing by the number of students for that option. Thus, in Example B1, the total marks on the whole test of the nine students who chose (b) were 289, so the mean for option (b) equals

$$\frac{289}{9} = 32.11.$$

Upper Group/Lower Group Percentages

The upper and lower groups are taken as being respectively the top and bottom 27% of students. In Example B1, 27% of 116 is 31.32. The top group may be taken as the 32 students who scored 37 or more; the bottom group as the 32 who scored 29 or less. The horizontal lines on Example B1 show the divisions between the groups.

EXAMPLE

B1   *Analysis of Multiple-choice Question*

Marks on   *Answers to this question*
whole test

x_T	*(a)	(b)	(c)	(d)	O	$f_p x_T$	$f_q x_T$
48	/					48	
44	卌					220	
43	////					172	
42	//					84	
41	/					41	
40	///				/	120	40
39	//					78	
38	卌 //	/				266	38
37	卌					185	
36	卌 //			//	/	252	108
35	卌 /	//		/	/	210	140
34	///			/		102	34
33	///	/		///		99	132
32				//			64
31	///	/	/	/		93	93
30	卌	//	//	////		150	240
29		/	/	/			87
28		/		///			112
27	//			///		54	81
26	///			/		78	26
25				///	/		100
24				/			24
23	//		/	//		46	69
22			//	//			88
21				/			21
20				/			20
n	64	9	7	32	4		
%	55.2	7.8	6.0	27.6	3.5		
Total						2298	1517
Mean-for-option	35.91	32.11	26.71	28.28	34.0	35.91	29.17
UG no.	30	1	0	0	1		
%	94	3	0	0	3		
LG no.	7	2	4	18	1		
%	22	6	13	56	3		

The number of students in the lower group should be the same as in the upper group; had there been more than three students scoring 29, it would have been necessary to exclude the extra ones from the lower group. If desired, the number in each group who chose each option may be calculated and converted to a percentage of the number in the group. In Example B1, 30 upper group students chose (a) and this is 94% of the group. Of the 32 lower group students, only seven (22%) chose (a).

Discrimination

Except for the approximate method (see page 217), calculation of the discrimination of an item requires a knowledge of the standard deviation, σ_T, for the whole test. For Methods 2 and 3 it is also necessary to know the test mean, M_T. In Example B1 the test mean was 32.89 and the standard deviation 6.21.

1. *General formula*—not the best method for manual analysis. The usually quoted formula for the discrimination, D, of a question is

$$D = \frac{M_p - M_q \times \sqrt{pq}}{\sigma_T}$$

where

M_p is the mean on the test as a whole of the students who answered the question correctly,

M_q is the mean on the test as a whole of the students who answered it wrongly,

p is the proportion of students who answered correctly (equal to the facility divided by 100),

q is the proportion who answered wrongly ($q = 1 - p$) and

σ_T is the test standard deviation.

However, for manual analysis it is better to use either Method 2 or 3 (described below); these require only one of M_p and M_q, in conjunction with M_T, which is the same for all questions in the test.

2. *Using M_p*—suitable for manual analysis if the mean of students answering correctly has already been found, with the means for other options (see *Mean-for-option* above) or if the students answering correctly are in the minority.

The formula is

$$D = \frac{M_p - M_T}{\sigma_T} \times \sqrt{\frac{p}{q}}$$

where the symbols are as defined for the general formula above and M_T is the mean of all students on the test.

To find M_p, the mean for students who answered correctly (i.e. the mean-for-option (a), if (a) is the key), use an $f_p x_T$ column as shown in Example B1. This gives the mark times the number of students gaining that mark, considering *only* those students who answered the question correctly. Thus all five students who scored 44 on the whole test chose (a) (5 × 44 = 220). Of four students who scored 40 on the whole test, only three chose (a) for this question, so the entry in the $f_p x_T$ column is 120. When the column is complete, add the entries in it to give $\Sigma f_p x_T$. The mean for students answering correctly, M_p, is then found from

$$M_p = \frac{\Sigma f_p x_T}{n_p}$$

where

x_T is the score of a student on the whole test,
$\Sigma f_p x_T$ is the sum of these scores for students who answered correctly and
n_p is the number of students answering correctly.

In Example B1

$$M_p = \frac{2298}{64}$$
$$= 35.91.$$

The proportion, p, of students answering correctly is equal to the facility divided by 100. In Example B1 $p = 0.55$, and $q = 1 - p = 0.45$.

The discrimination, D, of the question shown in Example B1 is then found from

$$D = \frac{M_p - M_T}{\sigma_T} \times \sqrt{\frac{p}{q}}$$
$$= \frac{35.91 - 32.89}{6.21} \times \sqrt{\frac{0.55}{0.45}}$$
$$= 0.54.$$

3. *Using M_q*—suitable for manual analysis if the facility is more than 50.

If M_p has not been found for other purposes (for example, if the means-for-options are not being calculated) and if the facility is greater than 50, it will be quicker to find M_q than M_p simply because fewer students are involved. M_q is the mean mark on the test as a whole of the students who answered wrongly the question under consideration. The procedure for finding it is similar to that for M_p, as described in Method 2; complete the $f_q x_T$ column, which shows test mark times number of students, considering *only* those students who got the question wrong. Add the figures in the $f_q x_T$ column to give $\Sigma f_q x_T$. Then M_q is found from

$$M_q = \frac{\Sigma f_q x_T}{n_q}$$

where

x_T is the mark of a student on the test as a whole and

$\Sigma f_q x_T$ is the sum of these marks for students who answered the question incorrectly and

n_q is the number of students answering incorrectly.

In Example B1 M_q is 29.17.

The discrimination, D, can then be found from

$$D = \frac{M_T - M_q}{\sigma_T} \times \sqrt{\frac{q}{p}}$$

where

M_T is the mean of all students on the test as a whole,

M_q is the mean on the test as a whole of the students who answered the question wrongly,

σ_T is the standard deviation of the test,

p is the proportion of students answering the question correctly (p is equal to the facility divided by 100) and

q is the proportion of students answering wrongly ($q = 1 - p$).

In Example B1, p is 0.55 and q is 0.45. The discrimination can therefore be found from

$$D = \frac{32.89 - 29.17}{6.21} \times \sqrt{\frac{0.45}{0.55}}$$
$$= 0.54.$$

5. *Approximate method*—suitable if a calculator is not available.

A simpler, but approximate, method of estimating the discrimination of a question is by reference to the numbers in the upper group and lower group who answered the question correctly. The formula is

$$D \simeq \frac{UG - LG}{n_{UG}}$$

where

UG is the number of students in the upper group who answered the question correctly,

LG is the number in the lower group who answered correctly and

n_{UG} is the number of students in the upper group.

In Example B1

$$D \simeq \frac{30 - 7}{32}$$
$$\simeq 0.72.$$

It will be seen that in comparison with the more accurate methods given in Nos. 1–3, the approximate method gives, in this case, a considerable over-estimate. In other cases the approximate method might underestimate the true discrimination, although for lower values of D the discrepancy would probably be smaller. The approximate method used to be advocated as being easier to calculate. Now that electronic calculators are available to assist in calculations, the advantage of the approximate method is generally outweighed by its inaccuracy.

Minimum Significant Levels of Discrimination

Although a figure of 0.2 is often quoted as the minimum acceptable value of discrimination for a question, the confidence which can be placed in the discrimination varies with the number of students on whom the analysis is

---

EXAMPLE

B2 *Minimum Acceptable Discrimination Figures*

No. of students	Point biserial		LG/UG method	
		Level of confidence		
	95%	99%	95%	99%
50	0.27	0.36	0.38	0.50
75	0.24	0.31	0.31	0.41
100	0.20	0.26	0.27	0.36
150	0.16	0.21	0.22	0.29
200	0.14	0.18	0.19	0.25
300	0.12	0.15	0.16	0.21

based. The larger the number of students, the greater the likelihood that the observed discrimination represents a genuine correlation between performance on the test and performance on the question under consideration; the lower the value of D, or the smaller the number of students, the greater the possibility that there is no genuine correlation and that the observed discrimination is due to chance.

Example B2 shows the minimum levels of discrimination which can be accepted as significant for given numbers of students. Figures are given for the point biserial method of calculation (Methods 1–3 described above are all variations of point biserial) and for the more approximate upper group/lower group method. Example B2 shows, for example, that, using the point biserial method, there is a 95% likelihood that a discrimination of 0.20 observed on 100 students represents a genuine and not a chance correlation; there is a 99% likelihood that this is so if the discrimination is above 0.26 for 100 students. Except for unavoidably small numbers, the 99% level of confidence should be sought.

This example shows that if the upper group/lower group method is being used, almost twice as many students must take the test in order for the same weight to be given to the values of discrimination obtained. This is not surprising when it is considered that only just over half of the test population are considered when calculating discrimination by this method.

C

Analysing Objective Questions other than Multiple-choice

This appendix describes the procedure for analysing multiple-response and matching questions. The procedure is very similar to that used for multiple-choice questions, as described in Appendix B, and is therefore explained in less detail here. The procedure for analysing assertion/ reason questions is exactly as for multiple-choice except that an additional option (e) must be considered.

Multiple-response Questions

The first stage is to prepare a matrix, as shown in Example C1. This is very similar to that used for analysing a multiple-choice question, but must also include a column (headed f_p) to show the number of students who answered the whole question correctly, since this information is not apparent from the rest of the analysis. The f_T column, which shows the distribution of marks of all students taking the test, is included in Example C1 for information only—it is not essential to the analysis of the individual question. It is, however, necessary to know the mean and standard deviation of marks for the total test; for Example C1 the mean (M_T) was 46.76 and the standard deviation (σ_T) 9.27. The lower group comprises the 25 students who scored 41 or below on the test as a whole; the upper group has 25 students with scores at or above 52, but excludes two students who also scored 52—in this instance the boundary of the upper group could not be made to fit neatly with the distribution of marks.

The *facility* of the question is found by counting the number of students getting the question completely correct and then converting to a percentage, i.e.

$$F = \frac{n_p \times 100}{n_T}$$

where

n_p is the number of students getting the question completely correct and n_T is the total number of students for the test.

In Example C1

$$F = \frac{42 \times 100}{91}$$

$$= 46.15.$$

Key and distractor performance are examined by counting the number of students selecting each option and converting to a percentage. Thus, in Example C1, 69 students (75.8%) chose (a), which was one of the keys; 23 students (25.3%) chose (d), which was one of the distractors.

Upper group/lower group performance on the question is examined by counting the numbers of each group who selected each option and converting to a percentage if desired.

The mean-for-option may be found, as for a multiple-choice question (see Appendix B) if required. This information is of no help in finding the discrimination of a multiple-response question.

Discrimination of the question may be found by first completing the $f_p x_T$ column. This shows the mark on the whole test, multiplied by the number of students who answered the question correctly. The column is added to give $\Sigma f_p x_T$. Then M_p, the mean on the test of the students who answered the question correctly, is found from

$$M_p = \frac{\Sigma f_p x_T}{n_p}$$

where

x_T is the mark of a student on the whole test,

$\Sigma f_p x_T$ is the sum of these marks for students who answered the question correctly and

n_p is the number of students who answered correctly.

EXAMPLE

C1   *Analysis of Multiple-response Question*

Marks on whole test			Answers to this question							
x_T	f_T	f_p	*(a)	*(b)	*(c)	(d)	*(e)	(f)	O	$f_p x_T$
77	/	/	/	/	/		/			77
71	/	/	/	/	/		/			71
67	/	/	/	/	/		/			67
65	/		/		/		/	/		
62	//	//	//	//	//		//			124
60	/	/	/	/	/		/			60
58	/	/	/	/	/		/			58
57	///	/	///	///	//	/	//	/		57
56	///	//	//	//	//		//		/	112
55	//	//	//	//	//		//			110
54	////	///	///	////	////	/	///	/		162
53	///	//	//	//	///	/	////			106
52	//	/	/	//	//		//	/		52
52	//	/	//	//	//	/	/			52
51	///	//	//	///	///		///	/		102
50	///	//	//	///	//	/	///	/		100
49	卌	//	//	////	///	/	////	//	/	98
48	卌	//	///	卌	////	//	////	//		96
47	//	/	//	//	//		/	/		47
46	卌	///	卌	卌	///	/	////	//		138
45	//	/	//	//	//	/	/			45
44	卌	///	卌	////	///	/	卌	//		132
43	////		///	//	///	//	///	///		
42	卌	//	///	////	///	/	////	/	/	84
41	///	/	///	///	/	/	///	/		41
40	//		/	//	/		//	//		
39	//	/	//	/	/		//	//		39
38	////	/	///	//	/	//	///	/	/	38
36	///		/	///	//	//	//	//		
35	///	/	///	//	/	//	//	//		35
34	////	/	////	///	/	/	////	///		34
32	/								/	
29	//		//	//	/	//	/			
25	/								/	
Total	91	42	69	76	63	23	76	33	6	2137
%		46.2	75.8	83.5	69.2	25.3	83.5	36.3	6.6	
UG		18	21	22	23	3	23	4	1	
LG		5	17	18	10	9	20	14	3	

In Example C1

$$M_p = \frac{2137}{42}$$

$$= 50.88.$$

The discrimination, D, is then found from

$$D = \frac{M_p - M_T}{\sigma_T} \times \sqrt{\frac{p}{q}}$$

where

M_p is the mean on the whole test of students who answered the question correctly,

M_T is the mean of all students on the test,

σ_T is the test standard deviation,

p is the proportion of students answering correctly (equal to the facility divided by 100) and

q is the proportion answering incorrectly ($q = 1 - p$).

In Example C1, $p = 0.46$ and $q = 0.54$ and

$$D = \frac{50.88 - 46.76}{9.27} \times \sqrt{\frac{0.46}{0.54}}$$

$$= 0.41.$$

Discrimination may also be found by the approximate method—

$$D \simeq \frac{UG - LG}{n_{UG}}$$

where

UG is the number of upper group students answering correctly,

LG is the number of lower group students answering correctly and

n_{UG} is the number of students in the upper group.

In Example C1

$$D \simeq \frac{18 - 5}{25}$$

$$\simeq 0.52.$$

Matching Questions

Only restricted analysis of matching questions is possible using manual methods or with a calculator. Using a computer it would, in theory at least, be possible to analyse the responses by finding the number of times each item in the first list had been matched with each item in the second. The resultant analysis would look rather like a separate multiple-choice analysis for *each* item in the first list in the question. However, such a mass of data would be difficult to interpret.

Without a computer, it is necessary to be content with examining those students who answered the question entirely correctly and those who answered incorrectly. A matrix is prepared, as shown in Example C2, showing students who answered entirely correctly (f_p), students who answered incorrectly (f_q) and omits (O). This question appeared in the same test as that shown in Example C1, so the test mean (46.76) and standard deviation (9.27) are the same. The columns are totalled.

Facility is found from

$$F = \frac{n_p \times 100}{n_T}$$

where
n_p is the number of students answering the question correctly and
n_T is the total number of students in the test.

In Example C2

$$F = \frac{63 \times 100}{91}$$

$$= 69.23.$$

The *upper and lower group performance* may be investigated by counting the number in each group who answered correctly, or incorrectly or omitted.

The mean on the whole test of those students who answered correctly (M_p) and the mean of those who answered incorrectly or omitted (M_q) may both be found if desired. In any case, one of these two figures will be required in order to calculate discrimination by the more accurate method. In Example C2 it is convenient to find M_q as fewer students are involved.

To find the *discrimination*, first complete the $f_q x_T$ column. This shows the test mark times the number of students who answered incorrectly or omitted the question. Thus, in Example C2, three students who answered incorrectly scored 35 on the test (3 × 35 = 105); of those who scored 34, two answered incorrectly and one omitted (3 × 34 = 102). Add the column to give $\Sigma f_q x_T$.

EXAMPLE

C2 *Analysis of Matching Question*

x_T	f_p	f_q	O	$f_q x_T$
77	/			
71	/			
67	/			
65	/			
62	//			
60	/			
58	/			
57	//	/		57
56	///			
55	//			
54	////			
53	//	/		53
52	//			
	/	/		52
51	///			
50	//	/		50
49	///	//		98
48	卌			
47	//			
46	卌			
45	/	/		45
44	////	/		44
43	//	/	/	86
42	////	/		42
41	//	/		41
40		//		80
39	/	/		39
38	///	/		38
36		///		108
35		///		105
34	/	//	/	102
32			/	32
29	/	/		29
25			/	25
Total	63	24	4	1126
UG	23	2	0	
LG	8	14	3	

M_q, which is the mean on the whole test of students answering this question wrongly (including omits) is found from

$$M_q = \frac{\Sigma f_q x_T}{n_q}$$

where
$\Sigma f_q x_T$ is the sum of their whole-test marks and
n_q is the number of such students.

In Example C2

$$M_q = \frac{1126}{28}$$

$$= 40.21.$$

The discrimination, D, is found from

$$D = \frac{M_T - M_q}{\sigma_T} \times \sqrt{\frac{q}{p}}$$

where
M_T is the mean of all students on the whole test,
M_q is the mean on the whole test of students failing to answer the question correctly,
σ_T is the test standard deviation,
p is the proportion of students answering the question correctly (equal to the facility divided by 100) and
q is the proportion failing to answer correctly ($q = 1 - p$).

In Example C2, $p = 0.69$, $q = 0.31$ and

$$D = \frac{46.76 - 40.21}{9.27} \times \sqrt{\frac{0.31}{0.69}}$$

$$= 0.47.$$

If the facility is less than 50, it is quicker to find M_p and use the formula as given for multiple-response questions (see page 223).

The discrimination may also be found by the approximate formula

$$D = \frac{UG - LG}{n_{UG}}$$

where

UG is the number of students in the upper group answering correctly,

LG is the number in the lower group answering correctly and

n_{UG} is the number of students in the upper group.

In Example C2

$$D = \frac{23 - 8}{25}$$

$$= 0.60.$$

D

Estimating the Mean and Standard Deviation for a Compiled Test

When an examination or test has been compiled from banked questions, the question analysis can be used to estimate in advance of the examination what will be the mean and standard deviation of students' marks. The purpose of this appendix is to explain how these statistics may be estimated.

After the test has been held the mean and standard deviation actually obtained may be compared with predictions. If there are differences they will be due, not to variations in the difficulty of the test or standard of marking, both of which are constant, but to differences in performance between the original and the new group of students. It should be noted, however, that if the numbers in the two groups differ considerably, or are both small, differences in analysis may be expected. In particular, a pretest conducted on a small sample will not give a good prediction of the performance of a larger student population. (See Chapter 16 for recommended size of pretest sample.)

Example D1 lists the facility and discrimination for each question of a 20-question in-course test. The questions have been arranged, as recommended, approximately in descending order of facility.

Estimating the Mean

In order to estimate what will be the mean mark for the test, add the facility values (F) of the questions to give ΣF. The mean, M_T, is then found from

$$M_T = \frac{\Sigma F}{100}.$$

In Example D1 the predicted mean is 11.72. This is the raw mean out of the total mark available (in this case 20). The percentage mean for Example D1 is 58.6%.

Estimating the Standard Deviation

If the facility values of the questions are mostly within about 10% of the average facility, it is usually satisfactory to estimate the standard deviation by an approximate method. This involves adding the discrimination values (D) for the questions to give ΣD. The standard deviation, σ_T, is then found from

$$\sigma_T = \Sigma D \times \sqrt{pq}$$

where
ΣD is the sum of discriminations of questions,
p is the proportion of students answering correctly a question of average facility (p is equal to the average facility divided by 100) and
q is equal to $(1 - p)$.

EXAMPLE

D1 *Estimation of Mean and Standard Deviation for a Compiled Test*

Question	F	D	$D\sqrt{pq}$
1	89	.29	.09
2	88	.26	.09
3	74	.21	.09
4	73	.28	.13
5	73	.15	.07
6	61	.27	.13
7	58	.34	.17
8	55	.32	.16
9	67	.21	.10
10	59	.18	.09
11	67	.22	.10
12	52	.35	.18
13	53	.15	.08
14	69	.49	.22
15	42	.24	.12
16	42	.29	.14
17	40	.25	.12
18	40	.32	.16
19	36	.17	.08
20	34	.28	.13
Total	1172	5.27	2.45

In Example D1

$$\sigma_T = 5.27 \times \sqrt{0.59 \times 0.41}$$
$$= 2.58.$$

This is equal to 12.9%.

If there is a wide spread of facility values, or if a particularly accurate estimate of the standard deviation is required, it is necessary to use a longer, more accurate method. This involves completing an additional column (as shown in Example D1) giving $D\sqrt{pq}$ for each question.

D is the question's discrimination,
p is the proportion of students answering this question correctly ($p = F/100$) and
q is the proportion answering incorrectly ($q = 1 - p$).

Thus, for Question 1 in Example D1,

$$D\sqrt{pq} = 0.29 \times \sqrt{0.89 \times 0.11}$$
$$= 0.09.$$

When the column is complete, it is added to give $\Sigma D\sqrt{pq}$, which is equal to the predicted standard deviation of the test, i.e.

$$\sigma_T = \Sigma D\sqrt{pq}.$$

In Example D1 the predicted standard deviation by this method is 2.45 or 12.25%.

E

Statistical Notation Used

Throughout the book, all symbols (for example, in formulae) are defined where they are used. For convenience, however, all the symbols used are defined in this appendix.

d the difference between a mark and the test mean

D the discrimination of a question

f frequency of occurrence of a mark

f_p frequency of a mark, counting only those students who answered correctly the question under consideration

f_q frequency of a mark, counting only those students who answered incorrectly the question under consideration

f_T frequency of a mark, counting all students who took the test

F facility of a question

k number of questions in the test

LG the lower group (i.e. the bottom 27% of students on the test) or the number within this group answering the question correctly

M a mean

M_p mean mark on the whole test of students who answered correctly the question under consideration

M_q mean mark on the whole test of students who answered incorrectly the question under consideration

M_T mean of all students on the whole test

n number of students

n_p number of students answering correctly the question under consideration

n_q number of students answering incorrectly the question under consideration

n_T number of students taking the whole test

n_{UG} number of students in the upper group

p proportion of students answering correctly the question under consideration

q proportion of students answering incorrectly the question under consideration

r reliability (of test)

UG the upper group (i.e. the top 27% of students on the test) or the number within this group answering the question correctly

x a mark

x_T mark of a student on the whole test

σ_T standard deviation of the test

Σ sum of, for example Σx_T is the sum of all marks on the test.

F

Keys to Examples

N.B. This list excludes some debatable questions which are discussed in the text.

Chapter 1
1.1   (c)
1.2   (b), (c), (d)
1.3   A2, B5, C1, D4
1.4   (a)
1.5   T
1.7   (d)
1.8   (b)
1.9   (a)

Chapter 2
2.1   (d)
2.2   (d)
2.4   (a)

Chapter 3
3.1   (b)
3.2   (d)
3.3   (b)
3.4   (b)
3.5   (d)

Chapter 4
4.1   (d)
4.2   (d)
4.3   (b), (d), (e)
4.4   (c)
4.5   A5, B2, C4, D3
4.6   F
4.7   T
4.8   F
4.9   F
4.10 F(a)

Chapter 6
6.2   (a)
6.3   (a)
6.4   (b)
6.5   (a)
6.6   (b)
6.7   (d)

Chapter 7
7.1   (c)
7.2   (d)
7.3   (a)
7.4   (a)
7.5   (d)
7.6   (a)
7.7   (a)
7.8   (d)
7.9   (c)
7.10 (d)
7.11 (b)
7.12 (a)
7.13 (d)
7.14 (d)
7.15 (c)
7.16 (a)
7.17 (d)
7.18 (b)
7.19 (c)
7.20 (b)
7.21 (b)
7.22 (a)
7.23 (a)
7.27 (a)
7.28 (d)
7.29 (a)
7.30 (a)
7.31 (c)
7.32 (c)
7.33 (d)
7.34 (b)
7.35 (d)
7.36 (d)
7.37 (b)
7.38 (b)
7.39 (b)
7.40 (a)
7.41 (c)

7.42	(c)	8.29	A4, B1, C2, D5	9.17	(d)
7.43	(a)	8.30	A4, B5, C1, D2	9.18	(d)
7.44	(c)	8.31	A3, B4, C2, D5	9.19	(d)
7.45	(b)	8.32	A2, B4, C1, D3	9.20	(c)
7.46	(d)	8.33	(b)	9.21	(c)
7.47	(d)	8.34	A3, B5, C1, D2	9.22	(a)
7.48	(b)	8.35	(b)	9.23	(d)
7.49	(b)	8.36	(c)	9.24	(b)
7.50	(d)	8.37	(a)	9.25	(c)
7.51	(a)	8.38	(c)	9.26	(b)
		8.39	(d)	9.27	(c)
Chapter 8		8.40	1B, 2C, 3A, 4D,	9.28	(d)
8.1	(b), (e), (f)		5E	9.29	(b)
8.3	(a), (e)	8.41	(d)	9.30	(a)
8.4	(a), (b), (d)	8.42	(d)	9.31	(b)
8.5	(b), (c)	8.43	(c)	9.32	(d)
8.6	(a), (b), (c), (e),	8.44	(c)	9.33	(d)
	(f)	8.45	(b)	9.34	(a)
8.7	(a), (b), (c), (e)	8.46	(d)	9.35	(b)
8.8	(b), (d), (f)	8.47	(d)	9.36	(a)
8.9	(d)	8.48	(a)	9.37	(b)
8.10	(b), (d), (e), (f)	8.49	(b)	9.38	(c)
8.11	(c)			9.39	(c)
8.12	(b), (d), (e)	*Chapter 9*		9.40	(a)
8.13	(c)	9.1	(b)	9.41	(c)
8.14	(a), (d), (e), (f)	9.2	(a)	9.42	(d)
8.15	(b)	9.3	(b)	9.43	(c)
8.16	(a)	9.4	(b)	9.44	(d)
8.17	(a)	9.5	(b)	9.45	(a)
8.18	(e)	9.6	(b)	9.46	(c)
8.19	(c)	9.7	(d)	9.47	(d)
8.20	(c)	9.8	(c)	9.48	(b)
8.21	(a)	9.9	(d)	9.49	(b)
8.22	(a)	9.10	(b)	9.50	(a)
8.23	(a)	9.11	(b)	9.51	(a)
8.24	(b)	9.12	(b)	9.52	(a)
8.25	A3, B1, C5, D2	9.13	(c)	9.53	(a)
8.26	A3, B1, C5, D3	9.14	(a)	9.54	(c)
8.27	A1, B5, C4, D2	9.15	(b)	9.55	(c)
8.28	A5, B3, C2, D1	9.16	(c)	9.56	(c)

9.57 (d)	9.72 (b)	9.87 (d)
9.58 (d)	9.73 (b)	9.88 (c)
9.59 (b)	9.74 (a)	9.89 (c)
9.60 (b)	9.75 (c)	
9.61 (b)	9.76 (d)	*Chapter 11*
9.62 (d)	9.77 (c)	11.3 (b)
9.63 (c)	9.78 (c)	11.4 (a), (d), (e), (f)
9.64 (a)	9.79 (c)	11.5 (a)
9.65 (d)	9.80 (c)	11.6 A2, B5, C1, D3
9.66 (a)	9.81 (c)	11.8 (a)
9.67 (a)	9.82 (c)	
9.68 (c)	9.83 (d)	*Chapter 15*
9.69 (c)	9.84 (c)	15.16 A3, B1, C2, D4
9.70 (d)	9.85 (b)	Other keys are as
9.71 (a)	9.86 (a)	shown in the question
		analysis.

Further Reading

Bloom, B. S. (ed.) *Taxonomy of Educational Objectives: The Classification of Educational Goals. Handbook I: Cognitive Domain* (London: Longmans, 1956)

City & Guilds of London Institute, Manual on Objective Testing (London: City & Guilds of London Institute, 1977)

Ebel, R. L. *Essentials of Educational Measurement* (Englewood Cliffs, New Jersey: Prentice-Hall, 1972)

Gronlund, N. E. *Constructing Achievement Tests* (Englewood Cliffs, New Jersey: Prentice-Hall, 1968)

Gronlund, N. E. *Stating Behavioural Objectives for Classroom Instruction* (London: Macmillan, 1970)

Hudson, B. (ed.) *Assessment Techniques: An Introduction* (London: Methuen, 1973)

Macintosh, H. G. *Techniques and Problems of Assessment: A Practical Handbook for Teachers* (London: Edward Arnold, 1974)

Macintosh, H. G. and Morrison, R. B. *Objective Testing* (London: University of London Press, 1968)

Nuttall, D. S. and Wilmott, A. S. *British Examinations: Techniques of Analysis* (Slough: NFER, 1972)

Rus, W. Bonney *Objective Testing in Education and Training* (London: Pitmans, 1973)

Index